PALEO SLOW COOKER

Slow Cooker Recipes Designed to Make Life Easier for You

(Diet on a Budget Without Going Broke)

John Frederick

Published by Sharon Lohan

© John Frederick

All Rights Reserved

Paleo Slow Cooker: Slow Cooker Recipes Designed to Make Life Easier for You (Diet on a Budget Without Going Broke)

ISBN 978-1-990334-09-2

All rights reserved. No part of this guide may be reproduced in any form without permission in writing from the publisher except in the case of brief quotations embodied in critical articles or reviews.

Legal & Disclaimer

The information contained in this book is not designed to replace or take the place of any form of medicine or professional medical advice. The information in this book has been provided for educational and entertainment purposes only.

The information contained in this book has been compiled from sources deemed reliable, and it is accurate to the best of the Author's knowledge; however, the Author cannot guarantee its accuracy and validity and cannot be held liable for any errors or omissions. Changes are periodically made to this book. You must consult your doctor or get professional medical advice before using any of the suggested remedies, techniques, or information in this book.

Table of contents

Part 1 1
Introduction 2
Chapter 1: Paleo Breakfast Slow Cooker Recipes 4
Be Our Guest Breakfast Meatloaf 4
Sweet Potato Pork Breakfast Casserole 6
Sausage and Butternut Squash Breakfast Casserole..... 7
Chapter 2: Beef-Based Slow Cooker Recipes 9
Spiced-Up Giardiniera and Italian Beef 9
Coffee and Jazzed-Up Beef Roast 11
St. Patrick's Paleo Corned Beef and Cabbage 13
Steamy Beef Stroganoff 14
Chapter 3: Pork-Based Slow Cooker Recipes 16
Cinco-Spiced Crockpot Pork Ribs 16
Vamos Carnitas 18
Aloha Hawaii Pulled Pork 20
Gala Apple Midwestern Pork Tenderloin 21
Chapter 4: Chicken-Based Slow Cooker Recipes 22
Honey-Dripped Chicken Wings 22
African Dance Moroccan Chicken 23
Athena Greek-Stuffed Chicken 25
Teriyaki Ginger Chicken 27

Balsamic and Peach Chicken Dinner 29

Chapter 5: Lamb-Based Slow Cooker 30

Spiced Lamb Roast 30

Coconut Craze Lemon Curry 31

Rosemary Leg of Lamb 33

Mechoui of Morocco Lamb 34

Chapter 6: Vegetarian Slow Cooker Recipes 35

Sweet Life Slow Cooker Sweet Potatoes 35

Curry-Green Bean Side Dish 36

Perfect World Paleo Lasagna 37

Paleo Smashed UP Cauliflower "Potatoes" 39

Chapter 7: Chilies, Soups, and Stews 41

Paleo Perfect Beef Chili 41

Meatball Medley Soup 43

Red Curry Beef Stew 45

Asian Bok Choy Pork Soup 47

Green Machine Pork Chili 48

Tropical Coconut Curry Sunny Winter's Day Pork Stew
.... 50

Utterly Kale-Full Chicken Soup 52

Puttering Paleo White Chicken Chili 54

Mighty Vegetarian Minestrone Soup 55

Better-Netter Butternut Squash Soup 57

Creamy Paleo Pumpkin Soup 58

Chapter 8: Paleo Slow Cooker Dessert Recipes 59

Autumn Arrival Apple Crisp.. 59

Very Berry Crumble.. 61

Impossibly Sweet Potato Brownies 62

Fall-Into-Pumpkin Pudding.. 64

Sweet Carolina Slow Cooker Applesauce 65

1. Slow Cooker Moroccan Chicken 66

2. Paleo Spicy Rib Appetizer 68

3. Crock Pot Pork Loin 70

4. Slow Cooker Rotisserie Chicken 70

5. Slow Cooker Butter Chicken 72

6. Slow Cooker Ham 74

7. Slow Cooker Jalapeño Popper Chicken Chili 74

8. Stuffed Peppers... 76

9. Crock Pot Chicken Fajita Bowl 78

10. Slow Cooker Turkey Meatballs 80

11. Fire Roasted Shrimp Tacos 82

12. Slow Cooker Chili 84

13. Texas Slow Cooker Beef Chili................................ 86

14. Slow Cooker Pumpkin Coconut Curry.................. 88

15. Whole Roast Chicken 89

16. Slow Cooker Cilantro Lime Pork Shoulder 90

17. 3-Ingredients Applesauce..................................... 91

18. Slow Cooker Maple Glazed Pecans 92

19. Salsa Verde Slow Cooker Chicken 92

20. Crockpot Minestrone Soup 95

21. Slow Cooked Turkey and Sweet Potato 96

Conclusion 99

Part 2 100

How to Make Paleo Condiments: 101

Paleo Mayonaise #1 102

Mayonnaise #2 103

Paleo Ketchup # 1 104

Ketchup #2 105

Homemade Paleo Worcestershire Sauce 106

Simple Mustard 107

Homemade Paleo Barbeque Sauce 108

Hot Sauce 109

Easy Paleo Horseradish 110

Paleo Horseradish with a Twist 111

Breakfast 112

Slow Cooker Sausage and Egg Soup 113

Slow Cooker Breakfast Pie 114

Paleo Slow Cooker Breakfast Casserole with Sweet Potatoes 115

Apple Breakfast Cobbler 116

Ham Egg and Spinach Breakfast Casserole 117

Slow Cooker Paleo Banana Bread 120

Gluten Free Smoky Bacon Wraps 122

Poultry 123

Slow Cooked Chicken Cacciatore 123

Hot and Zesty Lemon-Turmeric Chicken and Vegetables
.... 124

Crock Pot Italian Chicken 127

Easy Whole Crockpot Chicken 128

Paleo Slow Cooker Sicilian Hens 130

Sri Lankan Slowcooker Chicken 132

Chicken In A Pot 134

Crock Pot Chicken Recipe 135

Honey Garlic Chicken Wings 136

Jamaican Jerk Chicken Wings 137

Paleo Style Buffalo Wings 139

Honey Turkey with Orange Cranberry Sauce 140

Slow Cooked Turkey With Sweet Potatoes 141

Slow and Easy Turkey Barbecue 142

Beef - Pork - Lamb 144

Slow Cooker Paleo Pot Roast 144

Slow Cooker Pear Ginger Pork Chops 148

Leg of Lamb Cooked Slow with Rosemary Lemon & Garlic 150

Paleo Jamaican Beef Pepper Pot 151

Malaysian Slow Cooked Beef Curry 154
Optional Ingredients: 155
Corned Beef and Cabbage Paleo Friendly 157
Serving Suggestions: 158
Slow Cooker Honey Barbecue Pork Spare Ribs 159
Crockpot Coffee Braised Chile Beef 161
Optional Ingredients: 162
Simple Crockpot Barbecued Spareribs 163
Slow Cooked Fruited Pork 163
Pulled Pork Crockpot Recipe 164
Irish Lamb Stew -- Crockpot Recipe 165
Paleo Slow Cooker Lamb Vindaloo 166
Slow Cooker Italian Beef Sandwiches 168
Seafood 170
Paleo Jambalaya Crockpot Soup 170
Optional Ingredients: 171
Key West Slow Cooker Citrus Fish 172
Manhattan Clam Chowder 174
Crockpot Fish Chowder 176
Florida Keys Fisherman's Stew 178
Slow Cooked Shrimp Creole 180
Crock Pot Shrimp Marinara Sauce 181
Crock Pot Fish Au Gratin 182

Appetizers 184

Slow Cooker Sweet and Sour Meatballs 184

Dipping Roast Beef & Gluten-Free Tortilla .... **Error! Bookmark not defined.**

Gluten-Free Paleo Style Tortillas Recipe .... **Error! Bookmark not defined.**

Part 1

Introduction

The Paleolithic lifestyle outlined in this recipe book is truly life-altering. Your days of counting carbohydrates, counting calories, and counting fat can finally come to an end as you return to what your body yearns to eat: the very things your ancestors ate some two thousand years ago. Our digestive system hasn't altered at all in that time, and because of this, your body cannot digest the crazy processed things you can find so easily at the grocery store. It simply hasn't evolved to eat donuts: that's why, in a nutshell, the perpetual obesity problem persists. Our bodies are simply ill equipped to handle everything we throw in them.

Proponents of the Paleolithic diet state that they have greater energy levels, healthy-looking hair, muscle growth that led to greater weight loss, an increased level of insulin sensitivity, a decrease in depression and anxiety feelings, and several other benefits. Your body begins working precisely as it's supposed to when you give it the food it needs.

The slow cooker is the perfect utensil to elevate your Paleolithic diet plan, as well, because the meat you'll be preparing really enriches in flavor the longer it cooks. Set aside the baby back ribs in the slow cooker for some eight hours, and you'll find them falling off the bone and ready for succulent eating when you return. All the flavors begin to assimilate together, work with each other, to form a sort of medley.

Oregano, basil, garlic, sweet potatoes—the flavor list is endless—orchestrate something very essential for your end-of-the workday routine. You'll find that while you were out living your very crazy life, your slow cooker was at home creating a masterpiece for you: something you could never have created yourself in your ramen-noodle-microwave-schedule lifestyle.

Begin to live well with these forty recipes. Create breakfast recipes for guests, find fruit and cocao-based dessert recipes for your next celebration, or soups and stews for your next sick day. Alternately, create the next game-day ribs, the next family gathering curry—or one of the many other options outlined in this recipe book. You can live an elevated lifestyle with the assistance of the Paleolithic diet and its marriage to the slow cooker. Create warmth and hearty happiness in your household. Don't wait to fuel yourself with flavor and nutrition!

Chapter 1: Paleo Breakfast Slow Cooker Recipes

Be Our Guest Breakfast Meatloaf

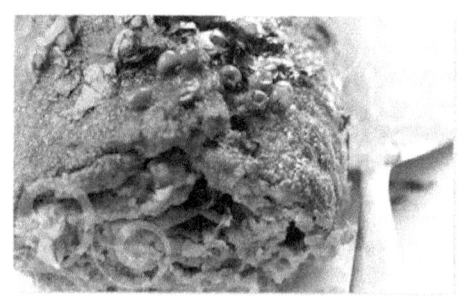

Prep Time: 10 minutes
Cook Time: 4 hours
Recipe Makes: 8 Servings
Nutritional Breakdown per Serving: 210 calories, 3 grams net carbohydrates, 19 grams fat, 22 grams protein

Ingredients:
1 ¾ pounds ground pork
1 tbsp. coconut oil
2 diced onions
½ cup almond flour
2 eggs
1 tbsp. garlic powder
3 tsp. fennel seeds
2 tsp. red pepper flakes

1 tsp. pepper
1 tsp. paprika
2 tbsp. maple syrup

Directions:

Begin by softening the onions in the coconut oil for about five minutes. Remove the onions from the heat and set them to the side. Next, bring together all of the other ingredients into a large bowl. Stir well in order to assimilate them. Toss in the onions and begin to fold and manipulate the meatloaf until you've created a loaf-like mixture. Pick up this "loaf" and place it in the center of the slow cooker.

Place the lid on the slow cooker and cook for a full three hours on HIGH.

Sweet Potato Pork Breakfast Casserole

Prep Time: 10 minutes
Cook Time: 8 hours
Recipe makes: 6 Servings
Nutritional Breakdown per Serving: 210 calories, 3 grams net carbohydrates, 18 grams fat, 24 grams protein

Ingredients:
8 eggs
1 shredded sweet potato
¾ pound diced pork sausage
2 tsp. basil
1 diced onion
1 tbsp. garlic powder
1 diced green pepper

Directions:
Begin by shredding the sweet potato in a food processor. Add the eggs to the slow cooker, first, and whisk them well with a fork. Next, add the spices and the prepared vegetables: basil, onion, sweet potato, garlic powder, and the green pepper. Stir the ingredients well, and finally add the pork sausage. Afterwards, place the lid on the slow cooker and cook for eight hours on LOW. Enjoy!

Sausage and Butternut Squash Breakfast Casserole

Prep Time: 10 minutes
Cook time: 10 hours
Recipe Makes 8 Servings
Nutritional Breakdown per Serving: 195 calories, 4 grams net carbohydrates, 16 grams fat, 14 grams protein

Ingredients:
¾ pound sausage
2 diced onions
12 eggs
1 ½ butternut squash
1 cup coconut milk

Directions:
Begin by browning the sausage in a skillet with a bit of olive oil. Dice up the onion and add the onion to the sausage. When the onion begins to look clear, pour the skillet's contents into the slow cooker.

To the side, mix together the coconut milk and the eggs.

Prepare the butternut squash be peeling it, de-seeding it, and slicing it up. Place the squash overtop the sausage and pour in the egg and coconut milk mixture.

Stir well and cook the casserole on LOW for ten hours. Enjoy.

Chapter 2: Beef-Based Slow Cooker Recipes

Spiced-Up Giardiniera and Italian Beef

Prep Time: 2 days
Cook Time: 8 hours
Recipe Makes 10 Servings
Nutritional Breakdown per Serving: 250 calories, 3 grams net carbohydrates, 27 grams fat, 20 grams protein

Giardiniera **Ingredients:**
2 cups diced carrots
2 cups chopped cauliflower
1 diced red pepper
3 sliced Serrano peppers

1 tsp. oregano
3 minced garlic cloves
½ cup apple cider vinegar
1 cup olive oil
1 tsp. thyme

Italian Beef **Ingredients:**
½ cup water
3 pounds beef pot roast
5 minced garlic cloves
1 quartered onion
1 tsp. thyme
1 ½ tsp. oregano

Directions:
Begin two days before you plan to create your Italian Beef recipe. You must bring together all of the chopped vegetables from the Giardiniera list in a bowl. Cover the bowl and allow it to refrigerate for a full twelve hours. Afterwards, mix together the vinegar, oil, thyme, and oregano. Pour this mixture overtop the prepared vegetables and stir well. Allow the vegetables to marinate for an additional twenty-four hours.

Eight hours before your marinade is completed, you can begin your Italian beef. Bring all of the beef ingredients into the slow cooker and allow all the liquid and herbs to coat the beef. Cook the slow cooker on

LOW for eight hours. When you're ready, serve the prepared marinade with the Italian beef. Enjoy.

Coffee and Jazzed-Up Beef Roast

Prep Time: 20 minutes
Cook Time: 6 hours
Recipe Makes 8 Servings
Nutritional Breakdown per Serving: 210 calories, 4 grams net carbohydrates, 15 grams fat, 15 grams protein

Coffee Rub **Ingredients:**
3 tbsp. ground coffee
1 tbsp. pepper
3 tbsp. paprika
1 tsp. Aleppo pepper
1 tsp. chili powder
1 tsp. ginger
1 tbsp. cocoa powder

Roast **Ingredients:**
1 ¾ pounds beef roast
1 cup beef broth
1 ½ cups pre-brewed coffee
3 chopped figs
3 chopped dates
1 diced onion

4 tbsp. balsamic vinegar

Directions:

Begin by bringing together the various spices and mixing them in a little bowl. Next, rub this mixture into the beef with a napkin or with your hand. Really dig into it, allowing the mixture to touch every surface.

To the side, combine the broth, coffee, dates, fibs, onion, and the vinegar in a food processor or blender. Create its liquid equivalent. Next, pour this created liquid into the slow cooker and place the beef on top. Cook on LOW for six hours. Afterwards, remove the beef and shred it with forks. Salt and pepper the result, and enjoy.

St. Patrick's Paleo Corned Beef and Cabbage

Prep Time: 20 minutes
Cook Time: 9 hours
Recipe Makes 8 Servings
Nutritional Breakdown per Serving: 240 calories, 2 grams net carbohydrates, 19 grams fat, 27 grams protein

Ingredients:
8 chopped carrots
1 wedged cabbage
3 diced onions
2 ½ pounds corned beef brisket
1 corned beef seasoning pack (found at local grocery store)
2 ½ cups water

Directions:
Prepare the vegetables and toss them in the slow cooker. Afterwards, place the beef in the slow cooker and sprinkle over the corned beef seasoning pack, making sure to get the mixture into every ridge of the meat.

Add the water to the slow cooker and cook on LOW for nine hours. Afterwards, serve the corned beef with the cooking juices from the slow cooker overtop. Enjoy!

Steamy Beef Stroganoff

Prep Time: 15 minutes
Cook Time: 8 hours
Recipe Makes 4 Servings
Nutritional Breakdown per Serving: 280 calories, 4 grams net carbohydrates, 24 grams fat, 27 grams protein

Ingredients:
1 pound sliced sirloin steak
2 diced onions
6 tbsp. coconut oil
1 ½ cups beef stock
8 ounces sliced mushrooms
3 minced garlic cloves
1 cup coconut milk
¼ cup white wine
salt and pepper to taste

Directions:
Begin by browning the sirloin steak in a bit of olive or coconut oil in a skillet. This should take about five minutes. Afterwards, place the meat in the slow cooker.

To the side, prepare the onions, mushrooms and the garlic cloves. Place this layer of vegetables over the sirloin. Pour in the remaining ingredients: coconut oil, coconut milk, white wine, and the salt and pepper. Stir well, and place the lid on the slow cooker. Cook on LOW for eight hours. Serve warm.

Chapter 3: Pork-Based Slow Cooker Recipes

Cinco-Spiced Crockpot Pork Ribs

Prep Time: 10 minutes
Cook time: 10 hours
Recipe Makes 12 Servings
Nutritional Breakdown per Serving: 275 calories, 2 grams net carbohydrates per serving, 27 grams fat, 32 grams protein

Ingredients:
3 ½ pounds pork ribs
2 tsp. garlic powder
2 tsp. basil
2 tsp. cumin
2 tsp. paprika
2 tsp. red pepper flakes
1 sliced jalapeno
3 tbsp. coconut aminos
2 tbsp. rice vinegar
1 ½ tbsp. tomato paste

Directions:
Begin by slicing the ribs into smaller pieces that you can actually stand up straight in the slow cooker. Prior to

actually doing this, salt them and pepper them. To the side, mix together the various other spices, and then massage the spices onto the ribs as well.

Place the sliced jalapeno at the bottom of the slow cooker, followed by the coconut aminos, the rice vinegar, and the tomato paste. Stir this concoction well. Then, stand up the ribs in the slow cooker so that they're not directly in the sauce. Place the cover on the slow cooker and cook on LOW for approximately ten hours.

Afterwards, remove the ribs from the slow cooker and keep them warm. Remove the fat from the slow cooker and bring the sauce in the interior of the slow cooker to boil. This will be your sauce for the ribs.

Also, if you want crispy ribs, you can toss your prepared ribs into the oven for ten minutes at 400 degrees Fahrenheit.

Vamos Carnitas

Prep Time: 15 minutes
Cook Time: 8 hours
Recipe Makes 8 Servings
Nutritional Breakdown per Serving: 245 calories, 3 grams net carbohydrates, 19 grams fat, 28 grams protein

Ingredients:
3 pounds pork roast
3 tsp. oregano
1 tsp. chili powder
2 tbsp. cinnamon
5 minced garlic cloves
juice from 2 oranges
juice from 2 limes
1 diced onion
3 tbsp. melted coconut oil

Directions:
Place the pork loin roast in the slow cooker and spread the chili powder and oregano all over the meat. Afterwards, place the garlic, onion, and the cinnamon on top.

Squeeze the oranges and limes on the top of the pork and allow the pork to cook on LOW for eight hours. Next, shred up the meat and melt the coconut oil on the stove. Make the carnitas crispy in the skillet for a delightful take on an old recipe.

Aloha Hawaii Pulled Pork

Pre Time: 5 minutes
Cook time: 8 hours
Recipe Makes 6 Servings
Nutritional Breakdown per Serving: 250 calories, 15 grams net carbohydrates, 22 grams fat, 26 grams protein

Ingredients:
3 ½ pounds pork shoulder
1 ½ cups cubed pineapple
3 tbsp. ginger

Directions:
Place the pork shoulder into the slow cooker and add the pineapple overtop the pork. Toss in the ginger and stir the ginger into the pineapple. Place the lid on the slow cooker and cook the pork on LOW for eight hours. Afterwards, shred the pork with two large forks and create your delicious pulled pork.

Gala Apple Midwestern Pork Tenderloin

Prep Time: 15 minutes
Cook Time: 8 hours
Recipe Makes 8 Servings
Nutritional Breakdown Per Serving: 240 calories, 15 grams net carbohydrates, 22 grams fat, 25 grams protein

Ingredients:
4 Gala apples
1 ½ pounds pork tenderloin
1 tbsp. nutmeg
2 tbsp. honey

Directions:
Begin by coring and slicing the apples and placing a layer of the apples at the very bottom of the slow cooker. Sprinkle the nutmeg over the apples. Next, place the tenderloin at the bottom of the slow cooker. Place another layer of apples over the tenderloin. Add a bit more nutmeg, if you please.

Place the lid on the slow cooker and allow the pork to cook for 8 hours on LOW. Enjoy both the pork and the apples on the side.

Chapter 4: Chicken-Based Slow Cooker Recipes

Honey-Dripped Chicken Wings

Prep Time: 10 minutes
Cook Time: 6 Hours
Recipe Makes 5 Servings
Nutritional Breakdown per Serving: 250 calories, 7 grams net carbohydrates, 18 grams fat, 27 grams protein

Ingredients:
30 wings
¾ cup liquid, raw honey
3 tbsp. olive oil
2 minced garlic cloves
salt and pepper to taste

Directions:
Place all the wings in the slow cooker and, to the side, mix together the olive oil, the minced garlic, the honey, and some salt and pepper. Drizzle this mixture over the wings in the slow cooker and stir well. Cook the wings on LOW for six hours.

African Dance Moroccan Chicken

Prep Time: 20 minutes
Cook Time: 6 hours
Recipe Makes 8 Servings
Nutritional Breakdown per Serving: 280 calories, 11 grams net carbohydrates, 18 grams fat, 35 grams protein

Ingredients:
14 ounces tomato sauce
1/3 cup pureed apricots
1 tsp. ginger
1 ½ tsp. cumin
juice from 1 lemon
4 minced garlic cloves
3 ½ pounds chicken breasts
½ tsp. paprika
2 diced onions
½ cup almond butter
2 cups water
3 tbsp. coconut oil

Directions:
Bring together the pureed apricot, tomato sauce, cumin, ginger, lemon juice, paprika, and salt in a small bowl. Stir. Afterwards, heat coconut oil in a skillet and allow it to melt. Place the chicken in the skillet and

allow it to scald a bit. Toss in the onions, ginger, and garlic and cook for two more minutes.

Pour this mixture into the slow cooker and add almond butter and water as well. Add all of the additional spices and stir. Allow the chicken to cook for six hours on LOW.

Athena Greek-Stuffed Chicken

Prep Time: 20 minutes
Cook Time: 8 hours
Recipe Makes 6 Servings
Nutritional Breakdown Per Serving: 250 calories, 3 grams net carbohydrates, 20 gram fat, 24 grams protein

Ingredients:
6 chicken breasts
1 tbsp. olive oil
2 sliced red peppers
1 diced onion
8 ounces spinach
1 ½ tsp. oregano
juice from 1 lemon
1 ½ cups chicken stock
¾ cup white wine
2 cloves minced garlic

Directions:
Begin by preparing the chicken. Slice the chicken in its side, creating a pocket. Salt and pepper the chicken and set them to the side.

Next, add the olive oil into a skillet and cook the onions and the peppers for about three minutes. Toss in the garlic and the spinach and cook for an additional one minute. Add oregano and remove the mixture from the heat.

Stuff the prepared pepper and onion mixture into each chicken and place each chicken in the slow cooker. Pour over the stock and the wine and allow the chicken to cook for eight hours on LOW. Enjoy!

Teriyaki Ginger Chicken

Prep Time: 5 minutes
Cook Time: 8 hours
Recipe Makes 6 Servings
Nutritional Breakdown Per Serving: 250 calories, 5 grams net carbohydrates, 18 grams fat, 22 grams protein

Ingredients:
1 ½ pounds chicken thighs
¾ cup coconut amino
2 tbsp. ground ginger
1 tbsp. honey
3 minced garlic cloves
salt and pepper to taste

Directions:
Begin by bringing together the honey, ginger, coconut aminos, and the garlic cloves. Stir well. Next, place the

chicken on the bottom of the slow cooker and pour the created sauce overtop.

Cook on LOW for eight hours and salt and pepper the chicken to taste. Serve warm.

Balsamic and Peach Chicken Dinner

Prep Time: 20 Minutes
Cook Time: 8 hours
Recipe Makes 10 Servings
Nutritional Breakdown Per Serving: 210 calories, 3 grams net carbohydrates, 15 grams fat, 18 grams protein

Ingredients:
3 tbsp. olive oil
2 diced onions
4 rosemary sprigs
3 pitted and sliced peaches
1/3 cup honey
10 chicken thighs
salt and pepper to taste

Directions:
Begin by heating olive oil and onions together in a skillet. When the onions have turned translucent, pour the mixture into the slow cooker. Add the rosemary sprigs, the pitted and sliced peaches, the honey, and the ten chicken thighs to the slow cooker. Salt and pepper the tops of the chicken, and attempt to coat the chicken with the sauce beneath it by turning it a few times. Cook on LOW for eight hours and serve warm.

Chapter 5: Lamb-Based Slow Cooker

Spiced Lamb Roast

Prep Time: 10 minutes
Cook Time: 7 hours
Recipe Makes 8 Servings
Nutritional Breakdown Per Serving: 210 calories, 2 grams net carbohydrates, 22 grams fat, 24 grams protein

Ingredients:
2 pounds lamb roast
8 ounces diced green chilies
2 diced green peppers
14 ounces diced tomatoes
2 tsp. garlic powder
1 tsp. chili powder
1 tbsp. cumin
salt and pepper to taste

Directions:

Place the lamb meat at the bottom of the slow cooker and add in the bell peppers, tomatoes, and the green chilies. Toss in the spices and stir well. Cook the meat on LOW for seven hours and serve warm.

Coconut Craze Lemon Curry

Prep Time: 10 minutes
Cook Time: 8 hours
Recipe Makes 3 Servings
Nutritional Breakdown per Serving: 210 calories, 2 grams net carbohydrates, 19 grams fat, 22 grams protein

Ingredients:
2 tsp. melted coconut oil
½ red chili
2 pounds diced lamb
1 diced celery stalk
1 tsp. turmeric powder
1 cup coconut milk
1 tbsp. tomato paste
¾ cup water
1 diced carrot
2 minced garlic cloves
3 tsp. garam masala

Directions:

Begin by pouring the coconut oil in a skillet and browning the lamb for five minutes. Afterwards, pour the lamb into the slow cooker and surround it with the vegetables. Pour over the coconut milk, the tomato paste, and the water, and add all the spices. Stir well. Place the lid on the slow cooker and cook for a full eight hours on LOW. Serve warm.

Rosemary Leg of Lamb

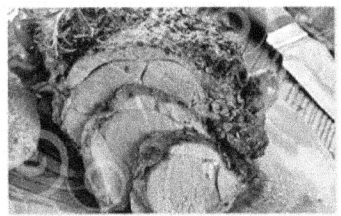

Prep Time: 5 minutes
Cook time: 8 hours
Recipe Makes 7 Servings.
Nutritional Breakdown per Serving: 240 calories, 2 grams net carbohydrates, 18 grams fat, 22 grams protein.

Ingredients:
1 leg of lamb
3 chopped rosemary sprigs
½ cup fresh mint
1 tbsp. olive oil
4 minced garlic cloves
salt

Directions:
Begin by completely drying out the leg of lamb. To the side, mix together the various herbs and the olive oil and stir well. Add this to the lamb and smear the lamb. Add salt. Place the lamb in the slow cooker and cook on LOW for eight hours. Serve warm.

Mechoui of Morocco Lamb

Prep Time: 15 minutes
Cook time: 8 hours
Recipe Makes 8 Servings
Nutritional Breakdown per Serving: 230 calories, 2 grams net carbohydrates, 22 grams fat, 23 grams protein

Ingredients:
1 lamb shoulder
4 tbsp. coconut oil
5 minced garlic cloves
1 tsp. pepper
2 tsp. salt
2 tsp. crushed saffron
2 tsp. cumin
¼ tsp. turmeric
1 ½ tbsp. olive oil

Directions:
Begin by mixing together the pre-melted coconut oil, garlic, pepper, saffron, cumin, turmeric, olive oil, and salt and pepper. Spread this mixture all over the lamb and place the lamb into the slow cooker. Cook on LOW for eight hours. Enjoy.

Chapter 6: Vegetarian Slow Cooker Recipes

Sweet Life Slow Cooker Sweet Potatoes

Prep Time: 5 minutes
Cook Time: 8 hours
Recipe Makes 10 Servings
Nutritional Breakdown Per Serving: 100 calories, 17 net carbohydrates, 0 grams fat, 2 grams protein

Ingredients:
5 sweet potatoes

Directions:
Begin by wrapping every sweet potato in a piece of foil and placing each potato in the slow cooker for eight hours on LOW. Afterwards, cut in halves and drizzle with a bit of almond butter or coconut butter to taste.

Curry-Green Bean Side Dish

Prep Time: 5 minutes.
Cook Time: 5 hours.
Recipe Makes 5 Servings
Nutritional Breakdown per Serving: 85 calories, 4 grams net carbohydrates, 8 grams fat, 3 grams protein

Ingredients:
5 cups kale
4 cups green beans
1 can vegetable stock
1 can coconut milk
1 ½ tbsp. yellow curry powder

Directions:
Pour the stock and the coconut milk into the slow cooker and stir in the curry powder. Afterwards, pour in the green beans and the kale. Stir well, and allow the beans to cook for five hours on LOW.

Perfect World Paleo Lasagna

Prep Time: 40 minutes
Cook Time: 7 hours
Recipe Makes 10 Servings
Nutritional Breakdown per Serving: 110 calories, 5 grams net carbohydrates, 8 grams fat, 3 grams protein

Ingredients:
5 minced garlic cloves
1 diced onion
14 ounces diced tomatoes
8 ounces tomato sauce
2 eggplants
3 cups spinach
½ cup pumpkin seeds
1 cup almond milk
2 cups walnuts
1 tsp. nutmeg
½ cup water
1 tbsp. olive oil

Directions:

Begin by slicing your vegetables. It's very important to slice your eggplant long-ways so that you achieve your "noodle" consistency. Next, slice up the onion and the garlic. Place the garlic, onion, and the olive oil in a skillet and cook them until the onions are clear. Add the diced tomatoes to the skillet and cook for an additional minute. Set this aside.

Create your fake cheese sauce by bringing together the pumpkin seeds, walnuts, almond milk, water, and nutmeg. Blend it completely to create a ricotta cheese consistency.

Next, prepare the lasagna in the slow cooker. Pour a layer of tomato sauce on the bottom of the slow cooker and then place down a layer of eggplant noodles. Next, add about half of the spinach to the lasagna. Add half of the fake cheese to the top of the spinach and then add the diced tomato, onion and garlic sauce. Repeat the layering system until you've run out of ingredients. Place the lid on the slow cooker and cook on LOW for seven hours. Enjoy.

Paleo Smashed UP Cauliflower "Potatoes"

Prep Time: 10 minutes
Cook Time: 8 hours
Recipe Makes 8 Servings
Nutritional Breakdown per Serving: 80 calories, 12 grams net carbohydrates per serving, 4 grams fat, 2 grams protein

Ingredients:
1 head of cauliflower
8 minced garlic cloves
1/3 cup chopped dill
1 tbsp. coconut milk
salt and pepper to taste

Directions:
Begin by placing the entire head of cauliflower in the slow cooker—without the leaves and stem. Here in the slow cooker, utilize a small knife to cut the cauliflower into its smaller florets. Toss the garlic and half of the dill into the slow cooker, as well, and add enough water so that some of the cauliflower pieces float. Cook on LOW for eight hours.

Afterwards, drain the slow cooker of the water and remove the remaining mixture. Place the mixture in a large bowl and add the "fresh" dill" and the coconut milk to the cauliflower. Puree the ingredients with a blender or a food processor and enjoy your Paleo mashed potatoes!

Chapter 7: Chilies, Soups, and Stews

Paleo Perfect Beef Chili

Prep Time: 1 hour
Cook time: 6 hours
Recipe Makes 15 Servings
Nutritional Breakdown Per Serving: 210 calories, 3 grams net carbohydrates, 19 grams fat, 22 grams protein

Ingredients:
4 ½ pounds ground beef
2 diced bell peppers
3 diced onions
4 diced yellow peppers
5 diced jalapeno peppers
3 diced poblano peppers
2 tbsp. oregano leaves
3 tbsp. cumin
3 tbsp. garlic powder
¼ cup beef stock
28 ounces diced tomatoes
2 tbsp. arrowroot powder mixed with 1 tbsp. water
¾ tbsp. cacao powder

Directions:

Begin by browning the beef in a bit of olive oil in a skillet. As it browns for about five minutes, begin chopping your vegetables.

Pour the meat into the slow cooker and follow it with your vegetables. Afterwards, sauté the prepared vegetables in the skillet for a moment—until the onions begin to become clear. Add the tomatoes and stir well prior to pouring the steaming mixture into the slow cooker.

Pour the beef stock into the slow cooker and add all the appropriate spices prior to cooking for 5 hours on LOW. Afterwards, add the arrowroot and water mixture along with the cacao powder and stir well. Cook for an additional hour and serve warm.

Meatball Medley Soup

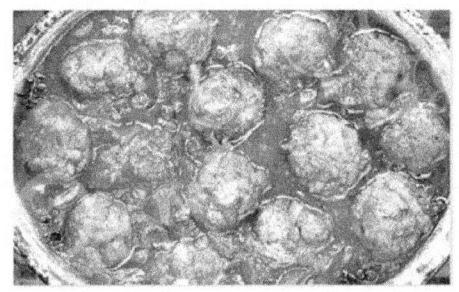

Prep Time: 10 minutes
Cook Time: 8 hours
Recipe Makes 4 Servings
Nutritional Breakdown per Serving: 275 calories, 5 grams net carbohydrates, 22 grams fat, 23 grams protein

Ingredients:
1 tbsp. olive oil
2 diced onions
3 minced garlic cloves
3 chopped celery stalks
15 ounces crushed tomatoes
1 tsp. oregano
14 ounces beef broth
1 egg
1 pound ground beef
4 tbsp. basil
1/3 cup almond meal

2 tsp. garlic powder
4 cups baby spinach
1 cup broccoli
1 cup cauliflower
1 sliced zucchini

Directions:

Begin by bringing together the celery and the onion in a skillet with the olive oil. Cook them for about ten minutes, until they begin to soften. Afterwards, add the garlic and cook for an additional minute. Pour this mixture into the slow cooker.

Next, pour in the beef broth, remaining vegetables, crushed tomatoes, oregano, basil, and salt into the slow cooker. Place the lid on the slow cooker and allow it to cook for three hours on HIGH.

To the side, as the soup cooks, you must make your meatballs. Stir together the egg, beef, oregano, pepper, and the garlic powder. Stir well and create meatballs. As you create each meatball, plop them into the humming soup. After you've finished allow the soup to cook for an additional hour on HIGH prior to serving. Enjoy.

Red Curry Beef Stew

Prep Time: 20 minutes
Cook Time: 8 hours
Recipe Makes 8 Servings
Nutritional Breakdown per Serving: 250 calories, 7 grams net carbohydrates, 22 grams fat, 23 grams protein

Ingredients:
3 tbsp. coconut oil
2 diced onions
2 ½ pounds beef stew meat
1 can coconut milk
2 tsp. peeled ginger
3 minced garlic cloves
½ cup red curry paste
3 cups chopped broccoli
juice from 1 lime
2 cups diced carrots

Directions:
Begin by placing the coconut oil in the skillet and browning the beef stew meat on all of its sides. Afterwards, transfer these pieces of meat to the slow cooker. Next, sauté the garlic, ginger, and onion in the skillet for an additional five minutes. Add the coconut milk in order to get all the "scum" off the bottom of the skillet.

Next, add the curry paste, lime juice, the tomato paste, and salt. Stir well, and pour this mixture overtop the meat in the slow cooker. Cook on LOW for eight hours and add the carrots and the broccoli with one hour remaining. Enjoy warm!

Asian Bok Choy Pork Soup

Prep Time: 5 minutes
Cook time: 8 hours.
Recipe Makes 2 Servings.
Nutritional Breakdown Per Serving: 215 calories, 3 grams net carbohydrates, 18 grams fat, 20 grams protein.

Ingredients:
3 cups Bok Choy (alternately, you can use spinach)
4 sliced scallions
1 pound pork
4 minced garlic cloves
4-inch section grated ginger
4 cups chicken stock

Directions:
Begin by pouring the chicken stock into the slow cooker. Toss in the grated ginger and the minced garlic. Next, cube the pork—if you're not using leftovers—and place this in the stock. Add the scallions, as well. Cover this mixture and cook the soup on LOW for eight hours.

When you decide you'd like to eat your soup, place the Bok Choy or spinach into a skillet with a bit of water. When the water begins to boil, add the pork from the slow cooker and sauté it until it's a bit browned. Bring the pork and the Bok Choy into the serving bowls and pour over the rest of the slow cooker broth. Enjoy.

Green Machine Pork Chili

Prep Time: 20 minutes
Cook time: 5 hours
Recipe Makes 8 Servings.
Nutritional Breakdown per Serving: 210 calories, 2 grams net carbohydrates, 20 grams fat, 22 grams protein.

Ingredients:
2 cups chicken stock
1 tsp. cumin
1 tbsp. cilantro
½ cup olive oil
6 minced garlic cloves
1 ½ pounds pork tenderloin
1 pound diced Anaheim chilies

½ tsp. oregano
3 diced jalapenos
1 diced onion
salt and pepper to taste

Directions:
Pour the broth, olive oil, cumin, and oregano into the slow cooker. Stir well. Afterwards, add the rest of the ingredients and set the slow cooker on HIGH. Cook for four hours. After those four hours, shred the pork tenderloin with two forks and allow the slow cooker to cook for an additional hour.

Tropical Coconut Curry Sunny Winter's Day Pork Stew

Prep Time: 15 minutes
Cook Time: 8 hours
Recipe Makes 10 Servings
Nutritional Breakdown per Serving: 275 calories, 5 grams net carbohydrates, 22 grams fat, 25 grams protein

Ingredients:
2 ½ pounds pork tenderloin
3 cups chopped carrots
1 cup pork or chicken broth
1 ½ pounds diced butternut squash
2 tbsp. curry powder
1 tbsp. apple cider vinegar
16 ounces coconut milk
5 minced garlic cloves
salt and pepper to taste

Directions:
Begin by placing the prepared butternut squash and carrots at the very bottom of the slow cooker. Dash with salt and pepper and place the pork tenderloin overtop the vegetables. Salt and pepper the pork, as well. Place the garlic on top of the layers.

Next, pour in the coconut milk, curry powder, and apple cider vinegar. Stir well. Add the broth and continue to stir. Cook the pork on LOW for eight hours. Afterwards, tear apart your pork utilizing two forks. Enjoy warm.

Utterly Kale-Full Chicken Soup

Prep Time: 30 minutes.
Cook Time: 6 hours.
Recipe Makes 6 Servings
Nutritional Breakdown Per Serving: 230 calories, 4 grams net carbohydrates, 12 grams fat, 22 grams protein

Ingredients:
5 cups shredded chicken
5 cups bone broth (or Paleo-friendly broth of your choice)
4 cups kale
4 lemons
1 diced onion
¼ cup olive oil
2 tbsp. lemon juice
Salt and pepper to taste

Directions:
Begin by washing and slicing the kale. Set the kale aside. Next, toss two cups of bone broth, onion, and olive oil into a blender and blend until the mixture is completely assimilated. Pour this creation into the slow cooker.

Next, add the next two cups of bone broth, the shredded chicken, kale, lemon zests, and lemon juice.

Salt and pepper the soup, and allow the soup to cook for six hours on LOW. Enjoy.

Puttering Paleo White Chicken Chili

Prep Time: 20 minutes
Cook Time: 6 hours
Recipe Makes 6 Servings
Nutritional Breakdown Per Serving: 210 calories, 2 grams net carbohydrates, 20 grams fat, 22 grams protein

Ingredients:
1 ½ pounds boneless chicken breast
2 diced onions
1 diced green pepper
1 diced onion
5 minced garlic cloves
1 tbsp. cumin
4 cups chicken broth
1 tsp. coriander
4 tbsp. coconut milk
3 tbsp. arrowroot powder
5 ounces green chilies
2 diced jalapenos

Directions:
Begin by slicing and dicing all the vegetables and the chicken. Add everything to the slow cooker and stir well. Place the lid on the slow cooker and cook on LOW for six hours. Shred up the chicken and serve it warm.

Mighty Vegetarian Minestrone Soup

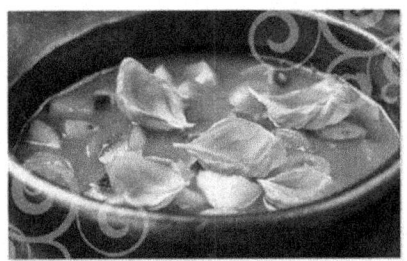

Prep Time: 20 minutes
Cook Time: 8 hours
Recipe Makes 8 Servings
Nutritional Breakdown Per Serving: 210 calories, 13 grams net carbohydrates, 3 grams fat, 5 grams protein

Ingredients:
1 diced sweet potato
2 diced carrots
2 diced zucchini squashes
½ cup spinach
29 ounces diced tomatoes
29 ounces vegetable broth
3 minced garlic cloves
½ tsp. cayenne pepper
1 tsp. oregano
1 tsp. parsley
3 tbsp. olive oil
salt and pepper to taste

Directions:

Begin by pouring the olive oil into the slow cooker and topping it with all the pre-cut vegetables. Pour in the vegetable broth and the tomatoes and stir well. Next, add the spinach and all of the spices. Stir well and cover the slow cooker. Cook on LOW for eight hours. Serve warm.

Better-Netter Butternut Squash Soup

Prep Time: 15 minutes
Cook Time: 8 hours
Recipe Makes 6 Servings
Nutritional Breakdown per Serving: 195 calories, 22 grams net carbohydrates, 9 grams fat, 4 grams protein

Ingredients:
5 cups diced butternut squash
1 diced onion
1 ½ peeled and chopped apples
2 minced garlic cloves
1 ½ tsp. dried thyme
½ tsp. sage
2 cups vegetable stock
1 ½ cup almond milk

Directions:
Bring everything except the almond milk together in a slow cooker and cook the soup on LOW for eight hours. After eight hours, pour in the almond milk and stir well. Pour the soup into a blender and puree the soup until you reach your desired consistency. Salt and pepper to taste, and enjoy.

Creamy Paleo Pumpkin Soup

Prep Time: 10 minutes
Cook time: 6 hours
Recipe Makes 5 Servings
Nutritional Breakdown per Serving: 150 calories, 15 grams net carbohydrates, 12 grams fat, 4 grams protein

Ingredients:
2 diced onions
2 cups vegetable broth
2 minced garlic cloves
4 tbsp. coconut oil
1 can coconut milk
1 tsp. cinnamon
1 tsp. allspice
1 tsp. nutmeg
salt and pepper to taste

Directions:
Begin by heating onions and garlic in coconut oil in a skillet over medium heat. The onions should become clear. Pour this mixture into the slow cooker. Follow the onion mixture with the vegetable broth, coconut milk, cinnamon, allspice, nutmeg, and salt and pepper. Place the lid on the slow cooker and cook on LOW for six hours. Serve warm.

Chapter 8: Paleo Slow Cooker Dessert Recipes

Autumn Arrival Apple Crisp

Prep Time: 15 minutes
Cook Time: 3 hours
Recipe Makes 4 Servings
Nutritional Breakdown per Serving: 170 calories, 11 grams net carbohydrates, 3 grams fat, 1 gram protein

Ingredients:
4 Gala apples
¼ cup shredded coconut
1/3 cup almond flour
1/3 cup sliced almonds
3 tbsp. cinnamon
Drizzles of honey

Directions:

Begin by peelings, coring, and chopping up the apples into small pieces. Layer the apples on the bottom of the slow cooker and sprinkle the apples with 1 tbsp. of the cinnamon.

Afterwards, mix together the slivered almonds, almond flour, remaining cinnamon, and the shredded coconut. Sprinkle this onto the apples and drizzle honey over the top. Cook the apples for a full three hours on LOW heat.

Very Berry Crumble

Prep Time: 5 minutes.
Cook Time: 2 hours.
Recipe Makes 5 Servings.
Nutritional Breakdown Per Serving: 280 calories, 10 grams net carbohydrates, 20 grams fat, 4 grams protein.

Ingredients:
4 cups frozen raspberries and blackberries
4 tbsp. melted coconut oil
1 ½ cups almond flour
1 tbsp. honey

Directions:
Begin by placing the various berries in the slow cooker and lending a single tbsp. of the coconut oil to the very center of the berries. To the side, mix together the coconut oil with the almond flour and the honey. Stir well until it begins to seem like almost-wet sand.

Sprinkle this mixture overtop the berries and cook the berry crumble on LOW for two hours.

Impossibly Sweet Potato Brownies

Prep Time: 20 minutes.
Cook Time: 2 hours
Recipe Makes 6 Servings
Nutritional Breakdown per Serving: 210 calories, 7 grams net carbohydrates, 13 grams fat, 4 grams protein

Ingredients:
3 eggs
1 sliced and diced sweet potato
¼ cup honey
¼ cup melted coconut oil
¼ tsp. baking powder
¼ tsp. cinnamon
2 tbsp. cocoa powder
4 tbsp. coconut flour
½ tsp. vanilla extract

Directions:
Begin by prepping the sweet potato by stabbing it a few times and placing it in your microwave for about fifteen minutes. Afterwards, peel it and mash it up. Stir in the rest of the ingredients: whisked eggs, melted coconut oil, vanilla, and honey. Stir well. Add the rest of the ingredients: cocoa powder, coconut flour, baking powder, salt, and cinnamon. Stir well.

Formulate each brownie into a ball—about one inch by one inch, and place each ball in the slow cooker. Place the lid on the slow cooker and allow the sweet potato brownie balls to cook for a full two hours on LOW.

Fall-Into-Pumpkin Pudding

Prep Time: 5 minutes
Cook Time: 7 hours
Recipe Makes 8 Servings
Nutritional Breakdown per Serving: 210 calories, 18 grams net carbohydrates, 23 grams fat, 8 grams protein

Ingredients:
4 tbsp. melted coconut oil
2 cups coconut milk
4 cups pumpkin puree
3 eggs
½ cup maple syrup
4 tbsp. coconut flour
1 ½ tbsp. vanilla extract
1 tsp. baking powder

Directions:
Bring all the ingredients into the slow cooker and stir well. Plop the top on the slow cooker and allow the pudding to cook for a full seven hours on LOW. The pudding will appear to have a crust, but it will be perfect beneath.

Sweet Carolina Slow Cooker Applesauce

Prep Time: 15 minutes
Cook Time: 3 hours
Recipe Makes 12 Servings
Nutritional Breakdown Per Serving: 120 calories, 18 grams net carbohydrates, 12 grams fat, 3 grams protein

Ingredients:
12 honey crisp or granny smith apples
3 tbsp. melted coconut oil
2 tsp. cinnamon
¼ tsp. salt
juice from 1 lemon

Directions:
Begin by placing the pre-melted coconut oil into the slow cooker. Spread this oil all over the slow cooker. Next, core, peel and slice up the apples. Layer the apples in the bottom of the slow cooker and then squeeze out the lemon onto them. Sprinkle over the cinnamon and the salt and stir well.

Cover the slow cooker and heat the apples on HIGH for two hours. Afterwards, stir and turn the slow cooker to low. Allow the apples to cook for an additional hour. Stir to achieve your desired applesauce consistency.

1. Slow Cooker Moroccan Chicken

Ingredients

2-3 pounds chicken thighs and drumsticks (I used 4 and 4)
1 TBS ghee or coconut oil
1/2 of a medium onion, sliced into half rounds
1 tsp cumin powder
1 tsp turmeric powder
1/2 tsp coriander powder
1 tsp cinnamon powder
1/2 tsp cardamom powder
Optional: 1/4 - 1/2 tsp cayenne powder
4 cloves of fresh garlic, minced
1 and 1/2 TBS fresh grated ginger
1 and 1/2 tsp unrefined sea salt
2 cups homemade bone broth
1 cup dried apricots, roughly chopped
2 cups sweet potatoes (or carrots or winter squash), cubed into bite-sized pieces
Garnish: fresh cilantro

Instructions

Combine cumin, turmeric, coriander, cinnamon, cardamom, and minced garlic (and optional cayenne) in a small bowl. Set aside.

Melt the fat of choice on medium heat in a large skillet and cook chicken pieces for 3 minutes on each side.

You may need to do this in batches if your pan is not big enough. Transfer into crock pot as you are done.

When chicken is done, add onions to pan and saute for 3-4 minutes. Add spice mixture and saute another 30 seconds to bring out the flavors. Add extra fat if it begins to stick. Turn off heat.

Add bone broth, ginger, and sea salt into skillet and then pour entire mixture mixture over the chicken in the crock pot.

Cook for 3 hours on LOW then add the dried apricots and chopped sweet potatoes (or carrots/winter squash). Cook for at least another 3 hours.

2. Paleo Spicy Rib Appetizer

Ingredients
3 lbs pork spare ribs
2 tbsp paprika
1 tsp chili powder
2 tsp cayenne
1 tsp sweet basil, dried
1 tsp cumin
Salt and pepper to taste after dish is cooked

For the sauce
1 cup tomatoes, peeled and chopped
2 serrano peppers, chopped and peeled
2 tbsp apple cider vinegar
3 cloves garlic, crushed
1/2 small onion, minced
1 tbsp fresh lime juice
2 pinches of salt

Instructions
Cut ribs into single pieces.

Rub pieces with the spices and place in the slow cooker.

Put tomatoes in a bowl, smash them with a fork and mix in the rest of the sauce ingredients.

Pour mixture over the ribs, cover and cook on low for 4 to 6 hours until ribs are tender.

3. Crock Pot Pork Loin

Ingredients
1 1/2 pound pork loin
1 can tomato sauce (15 oz)
2 medium zucchini, sliced
1 head   cauliflower, separated into medium florets
2 tablespoon basil, dried
1/4 teaspoon black pepper, freshly ground
1/2 teaspoon sea salt, (optional)

Instructions
Add all of the ingredients to a large crock pot.

Cook on high for 3-4 hours or low 7-8 hours.

4. Slow Cooker Rotisserie Chicken

Ingredients
1 whole chicken (4-5 lbs.), rinsed and patted dry
2 Tbsp. extra virgin olive oil
1 tsp. dried thyme
1 tsp. garlic powder
1 tsp. sea salt
1 tsp. paprika
1 tsp. ground black pepper
1/2 tsp. cayenne pepper (optional)

Instructions

Make about 6 balls of aluminum foil and line the bottom of your slow cooker with them (you don't have to crunch the balls up too tight). You can also substitute chopped vegetables such as onion, carrots and celery if you don't want to use aluminum foil, or get one of these handy slow-cooker roasting racks that helps keep items elevated while cooking.

Combine the thyme, garlic powder, paprika, salt and pepper in a small bowl. Rub the oil all over the chicken, then and rub the seasoning over, making sure the chicken is evenly coated.

Place chicken in the crock pot on top of the chopped vegetables. Cook on low for 6-8 hours or until chicken is cooked through.

As an optional finishing step, place the oven rack in the bottom third of the oven and turn the oven on to broil. Carefully place the chicken in a baking dish and allow to broil for about 5-10 minutes until the skin is crispy and brown.

5. Slow Cooker Butter Chicken

Ingredients
1 Tbsp Organic Coconut Oil
3 - 4 whole Garlic, crushed
1 whole Onion, diced
1 3/4 cup Coconut Milk
3/4 cup Tomato Paste
2 Tbsp Arrowroot Flour
2 tsp Garam Masala
1 tsp Curry Powder
1/2 tsp ground Ginger
1/2 tsp Chili Powder, Add more if you like it hotter
1 pinch Sea Salt
1 pinch Black Pepper
2 1/5 lb Skinless Chicken Breast

Instructions
Heat coconut oil in a large saucepan on medium high heat.

Add onion and garlic, cook, stirring frequently for approximately 3 minutes or until the onions have become translucent.

Add coconut milk, tomato paste, tapioca flour, garam masala, curry powder, ginger powder, chili powder and ginger powder, stirring until well combined and the sauce has started to thicken.

Season with salt and pepper.

Add chicken to the slow cooker, then add the sauce and mix through the chicken. Cover and cook on low heat for 5 hours.Cover and cook on low heat for 5 hours.

Serve with coriander and your favourite side.

6. Slow Cooker Ham

Ingredients
1 4-6 lb Ham Roast
1/4 cup Honey
1/2 cup Orange Juice
2 tsp Dried Rosemary
4 tbs Coconut Oil
Zest of 1 Orange
1 tbs Apple Cider Vinegar

Instructions
Place ham in slow cooker.

Put the rest of the ingredients on the ham.

Cook on low for 4-6 hours.

7. Slow Cooker Jalapeño Popper Chicken Chili

Ingredients
1 medium white onion, diced
3 cloves minced garlic
1 red bell pepper, diced
2 jalapeños, seeds removed
1 large sweet potato, 14 oz
1 lb 93% lean ground chicken
1 lb 95% lean ground beef
2 tsp smoked paprika

2 tsp chili powder
2 tsp dried oregano
2 tsp kosher salt
1 tsp ground cumin
1/4 tsp red pepper flakes
1 (14 oz) can petite diced tomatoes
1 cup reduced sodium chicken broth
chopped scallions, for garnish
8 oz diced avocado (from 2 small haas)
4 oz goat cheese (optional)

Instructions

Place all the ingredients except the scallion, avocado and goat cheese in the slow cooker and cook on low 8 hours. When done, break up the ground meat with a wooden spoon and add half of the goat cheese if using.

Serve garnished with scallions and avocado on top.

8. Stuffed Peppers

Ingredients

4 bell peppers
1 lb ground meat
1/2 head of cauliflower
1 onion, diced
1 carrot, diced
4 cloves of garlic, minced
6 ounces tomato paste
1/4 cup homemade italian seasoning blend (equal parts marjoram, thyme, rosemary, savory, sage, oregano, basil)
salt and pepper to taste
1/4 cup beef stock

Instructions

Pulse your cauliflower, onion, carrots, and garlic in the food processor to blend as fine as possible. Do it seperately if your food processor isn't large enough. If you don't own one you can dice everything as small as possible by hand.

Cut the tops off of your peppers, keeping them intact and clean the seeds out.

Mix your vegetables in a mixing bowl with your meat, tomato paste, seasonings and salt and pepper.

Once all ingredients are combined well, spoon the mixture into your peppers and level off at the top of the pepper.

Place the peppers in your crock pot and put the tops of the peppers on them.

Pour your liquid in the bottom of the crock pot and cook on low for 6-8 hours.

9. Crock Pot Chicken Fajita Bowl

Ingredients

For the marinade
4 boneless, skinless chicken breasts
1/2 cup extra-virgin olive oil
2 tablespoons red wine vinegar
Juice of 1 lime
1 teaspoon powdered garlic

Vegetables and Spices
2 yellow onions, sliced thin
2 green bell peppers, sliced thin
2 red bell peppers, sliced thin
2 teaspoons powdered garlic
2 teaspoons ground cumin
1 (15.5 ounce) jar organic salsa

Toppings (optional)
Sour Cream (omit for Paleo)
Chopped Cilantro
Chopped Avocado
Lime wedges, for spritzing
Shredded Cheddar cheese (omit for Paleo)

Instructions
Place chicken in a baking dish. Whisk olive oil, red wine vinegar, lime juice and garlic powder in a small

measuring cup. Pour olive oil mixture over the chicken. Cover and place in the fridge to marinate overnight.

The next morning, place onions and bell peppers in the bottom of a slow cooker. Sprinkle the powdered garlic and cumin over the vegetables.

Place the chicken on top of the vegetables and pour marinade over it all. Pour the salsa evenly over the chicken. Put the lid on, and cook on low for 7-8 hours until chicken is cooked through and fork tender.

Remove chicken and shred. Serve chicken with peppers and toppings.

10. Slow Cooker Turkey Meatballs

Ingredients

1 lb ground turkey
1 lb turkey sausage (ground or in casing)
1 tsp basil
1/2 tsp oregano
1/2 tsp rosemary
1/2 tsp thyme
1/2 tsp onion powder
1/2 tsp garlic powder
1 tsp salt
1/2 cup almond meal
1 egg, beaten
24 oz San Marzano crushed tomatoes
1/2 large onion, quartered
2 cloves garlic, crushed
2 tbsp red wine vinegar

Instructions

Begin by heating a large skillet to medium high.

In a large bowl, mix together both ground turkey and sausage until well blended.

In a separate small bowl, mix together basil, oregano, rosemary, garlic powder, onion powder, salt, and almond meal. Add mixture to the meat.

With your hands, mix together the spices and meat until well incorporated. Add in beaten egg and continue to mix well.

Form meat mixture into large meatballs (about 1.5-2 inches in diameter).

Grease your skillet, and add meatballs. Cook each meatball about 1 minute per side until the meat is browned (but not cooked through). Add meatballs to slow cooker.

Top meatballs with tomatoes, onion, garlic, and vinegar.

Cook on low for 5-6 hours.

Serve plain with fresh basil, or with spaghetti squash.

11. Fire Roasted Shrimp Tacos

Ingredients

11 oz medium peeled frozen raw shrimp
14.5 oz can fire roasted stewed tomatoes
2 tbsp spicy salsa
5 oz or 1/2 cup chopped bell pepper
dash of sea salt and black pepper
1/2 tsp cumin
1/4 to 1/2 tsp chili pepper or cayenne pepper
1/2 tsp minced garlic
3-4 tbsp chopped cilantro (2 tbsp goes on top)
1-2 tbsp olive oil
optional toppings - feta, avocado, chili pepper, etc.

Instructions

Layer your raw frozen shrimp at the bottom of pot. drizzle with 1 tbsp olive oil.

Add in your sea salt and pepper and mix around shrimp. If you are using frozen shrimp, then drain your tomato juice first, then add in your tomatoes and the rest of your ingredients, including your seasoning.

Mix again and cook in crock pot on low for 3-4 hrs. Or high for 2 hours.

Note that 2 tbsp cilantro goes in the mix and 1-2 tbsp on top for garnish.

Serve with gluten free corn or paleo tortillas, rice, and avocado!

12. Slow Cooker Chili

Ingredients

1 pound of organic grass-fed ground beef

1 medium white onion, diced

3 cloves of garlic, minced

28 ounce can of organic fire roasted diced tomatoes

6 ounce can of organic tomato paste +2 cans of filtered water (1/2 cup)

1 package of preservative & sugar free bacon, sliced into small pieces (see notes)

3 tablespoons of chili powder

1 tablespoon of oregano

1 tablespoon of basil

2 teaspoons of cumin

1 teaspoon garlic powder

1 teaspoon dehydrated onion

1/2 teaspoon of Cayenne powder

1/4 teaspoon smoked Paprika

Salt and pepper to taste

Instructions

Cook bacon pieces and ground beef over medium-high heat until they just begin to brown.

Add onion and lower heat to medium, cover pan and cook, stirring occasionally, until translucent, about 4 to 5 minutes.

Uncover pan and add garlic, cook 1 to 2 minutes.

Drain some of the liquid out of the pan and transfer the mixture to your crockpot.

Add the rest of the ingredients to your crockpot and stir them until mixed well.

Set your crockpot to low add the lid and cook for about 8 to 10 hours.

Spoon chili into bowls, or spoon inside of pasture raised hot dogs.

Garnish with your favorite toppings.

13. Texas Slow Cooker Beef Chili

Ingredients
1 pound grass-fed organic beef
1 green bell pepper, seeded and diced
1 large onion, diced
4 large carrots chopped small
26 oz finely chopped tomatoes
1/2 teaspoon sea salt
1 teaspoon onion powder
1 tablespoon chopped fresh parsley
1 tablespoon Worcestershire sauce
4 teaspoons chili powder
1 teaspoon paprika
1 teaspoon garlic powder
Pinch of cumin

Optional Toppings
Dairy-free sour cream
Diced onions
Sliced Jalapeños

Instructions
Place the ground beef in a medium-size skillet over high heat and brown, stirring, until no longer pink.

Spoon it into your slow cooker, including the fat.

Place the green bell pepper, onion, carrots and tomatoes into the slow cooker.

Stir all the ingredients well, then add the remaining spices and seasonings.

Stir once more, cover and cook on low for 8 hours or on high for 5 hours.

Top with dairy-free sour cream if desired, additional diced onions or jalapeños.

14. Slow Cooker Pumpkin Coconut Curry

Ingredients

1 15-ounce can of unsweetened coconut milk (full fat, not light)
2 cups pumpkin puree (not pumpkin pie filling)
1 cup chicken stock
1/2 tablespoon curry powder
1/4 teaspoon tumeric powder
2 teaspoon garam masala
1/2 teaspoon Kosher salt
1/4 teaspoon ground black pepper
1/2 large onion, diced
1 garlic clove, minced
3 carrots, cut into 1-inch pieces
3 cups 1-inch cubed sweet potatoes
2 chicken breasts, cut into 1-inch cubes
Juice of 1 lime

Instructions

In the insert of a 4-quart or larger slow cooker, add the coconut milk, pumpkin puree, chicken stock, curry powder, tumeric powder, garam masala, salt, and pepper.

Whisk together to make sure it is all combined and spices are evenly distributed.

Add the onion, garlic, carrots, sweet potatoes, chicken breasts, and lime juice to the mixture.

Stir to coat and incorporate.

Cook on low for 6 hours.
Serve over rice.

15. Whole Roast Chicken

Ingredients
1 whole, organic chicken (about 4-5 lbs)
2 tsp Celtic salt
1 tsp organic white pepper
1/2 tsp organic black pepper, freshly ground
1 tsp organic cayenne pepper
2 tsp organic paprika
1/2 tsp organic garlic powder
3 sprigs of fresh rosemary (or 1 tsp dried rosemary)
1 large onion, loosely chopped

Instructions
Combine all spices in a small bowl and set aside.

Remove the giblets from the chicken.

Put onions in the bottom of the crockpot. (Don't add liquid. The onions keep the chicken from sticking to the bottom and will add a bit of moisture to the chicken.)

Add chicken and potatoes in the crockpot.

Rub the top and sides of chicken with spices.

Cook on low for 5-6 hours.

When done, check to make sure chicken is cooked all the way through.

Save the liquid and bones from the chicken to make a delicious bone broth later.

16. Slow Cooker Cilantro Lime Pork Shoulder

Ingredients
1 cup fresh cilantro
1/2 cup fresh mint
3 tablespoons lime zest (or 3 limes)
1 tablespoon lime juice (juice of 1 lime)
3-4 cloves garlic
1 tablespoon olive oil
1 tablespoon sea salt
2-3 pound pork shoulder (Boston Butt)

Instructions
Add all ingredients (except the pork shoulder) to the bowl of a large food processor.

Process on medium speed until pulverized and evenly blended, about to the consistency of pesto. Spread the mixture over the pork shoulder, wrap it in plastic, and place it in the refrigerator to marinate for at least 8 hours, and up to 24 hours.

Place the marinated pork shoulder in a slow cooker. You don't need to add anything else, just the marinated roast. Place the lid on the slow cooker and turn the temperature to low. Cook for 10-14 hours.

After cooking, remove the pork shoulder to a plate or serving platter and let stand for ten minutes before shredding/slicing and serving.

17. 3-Ingredients Applesauce

Ingredients
1 tablespoon coconut oil
6-8 large sweet baking apples
1 cinnamon stick

Instructions
Oil crock pot with coconut oil.

Core, peel, and quarter apples. Add to crock pot with cinnamon stick.

Cook on low 6-8 hours, until soft. Remove cinnamon stick.

Mash apples or puree with immersion blender.

18. Slow Cooker Maple Glazed Pecans

Ingredients

3 cups raw pecans

1/4 cup maple syrup

2 tsp ground vanilla beans (vanilla extract would probably work as well)

1 tsp sea salt

1 T coconut oil

Instructions

Throw all the ingredients in a crock pot

Cook on low for a 1-3 hours making sure to stir often.

Store them in a mason jar after they have cooled completely.

19. Salsa Verde Slow Cooker Chicken

Ingredients

1 large onion, sliced

6 to 8 cloves of garlic, smashed

24 oz jar roasted salsa verde

4 pounds organic boneless, skinless chicken breasts

2 Tablespoons Kasandrinos Extra Virgin Olive Oil
1 Tablespoon paprika
2 teaspoons cumin
2 teaspoons coriander
2 teaspoons sea salt
1 teaspoon black pepper
2 bay leaves
1/3 to 1/2 cup chicken broth
1/4 cup tomato paste (for sauce)

Instructions
Add the sliced onion and smashed garlic to the bottom of the slow cooker. These are going to be the base flavor of the dish.

Place the chicken breasts on top of the onion and garlic. Pour the jar of roasted salsa verde over the chicken.

Add 2 tbsp of extra virgin olive oil to the slow cooker. Add the remaining spices: paprika, cumin, coriander, sea salt, pepper, and bay leaves.
Mix around all of the ingredients in the slow cooker. You want to make sure you have enough liquid, but keep in mind that the onions (veggies, in general) and the chicken will give off some liquid. Add about 1/3 to 1/2 of chicken broth for good measure.

Cover and turn the slow cooker on HIGH for 6 hours, but check on the chicken after 4 hours.

At 4 hours, remove the big chunks of chicken and allow the liquid to continue to reduce down for 2 more hours.

Once chicken is cooled, shred by hand or by using 2 forks.

For the sauce

Take the liquid from the slow cooker, 1/2 at a time, and add to a Vitamix (or similar blender). When blending a hot liquid, only fill your blender halfway to avoid splattering that hot liquid everywhere.

Don't forget to remove the centerpiece from the blender to allow steam to escape. Use an old kitchen towel (or two!) to cover the open hole of the blender, while still allowing steam to escape.

Then, pour the liquid into a cast iron dutch oven. Simmer and reduce the liquid. This will create more of a sauce texture.

Once reduced, whisk in the tomato paste. This will add a great flavor, but you will want to season with more salt and pepper, to your own taste. Continue to whisk until well combined. Cover and allow to simmer until desired consistency.

20. Crockpot Minestrone Soup

Ingredients
2 Tbsp Olive Oil
1 Yellow Sweet Potato, diced
1 cup Carrots, diced
2 Celery Stalks, diced
2 Zucchini Squash, diced
2 Shallots, diced
2 cloves Garlic, minced
28 oz Chicken or Vegetable Broth
28 oz can Diced Tomatoes w/ Juice
1/2 cup Frozen Spinach -or- 1 cup packed Fresh Spinach, chopped
2 Bay Leaves
2 tsp Oregano
1 tsp Basil
1 tsp Parsley
1/4 tsp Cayenne Pepper
1/4 tsp Sea Salt
1-1/2 lb Ground Pork Sausage (optional)

Instructions
Place the olive oil in the bottom of the crock pot.

Add the prepared sweet potatoes, carrots, celery, zucchini, shallots, and garlic to the crock pot.

Pour in the chicken (or vegetable) broth. Add the entire can (including juice) of diced tomatoes.

Add the frozen spinach (no need to thaw and drain, just add it frozen).

Add in the oregano, basil, parsley, cayenne, and salt.

Stir everything together, add the bay leaved, cover, and cook on low for 6-8 hours.

About 2 hours before the soup is done, brown the ground pork sausage, breaking it up into small pieces with the back of a wooden spoon.

Once the pork is cooked through (no pink), add it to the crock pot and mix it all together.
Remove bay leaves before serving.

21. Slow Cooked Turkey and Sweet Potato
Ingredients
2 lbs. of ground turkey
2 medium sweet potatoes, diced
1 cup baby carrots, chopped
2 15-oz cans of organic diced tomatoes
1 red onion, diced

1 cup green onions, chopped
4 garlic cloves, finely diced
1 tablespoon honey
1 teaspoon ground cumin
2 tablespoons chili powder
1/4 teaspoon cayenne pepper
1 teaspoon sea salt
1 cup filtered water (plus 1/4 cup for cooking the ground turkey)

Instructions
Prep all of your ingredients ahead of time.

Place ground turkey in your cooking pan and, using your wooden spoon, help break the ground turkey.

Add in 1/4 cup of filtered water and cover the pan with lid. Place pan under medium heat and cook until meat is no longer pink (around 8-10 minutes). Be sure to stir the turkey around to prevent it from burning.

Add cooked turkey to crockpot. Then add: remaining filtered water, garlic, red onion, green onion, diced tomatoes, sweet potatoes, carrots, honey, and spices. Mix ingredients well and cover crockpot with lid.

Plug in your crockpot and set it to cook on low for 7 hours.

Serve stew and it top with diced avocados or with your favorite herb.

Conclusion

This book takes you on a journey to better nutritive understanding. Armed with the forty recipes, you can truly take hold of your life and your schedule once more. You can toss a few funny-looking naked ingredients into a slow cooker in the morning and come home to a full-blown feast in the evening. While you're out living your crazy life, your body will be reaping the rewards of the essential nutrients brought in by your new Paleo lifestyle. You'll lose weight, build muscle, relieve anxiety, and find greater reason to fuel yourself well. Find reasons to utilize the slow cooker this fall and this winter. Your soul—and your waistline—will thank you.

Part 2

Chinese Food Substitutes

Substitutes for non-paleo: soy sauce, hoisin sauce, rice vinegar.

* Try fish sauce instead of soy sauce; it has a similar flavor.

* Toasted sesame oil can give the flavor you are looking for as well.

* Coconut animos to replace soy sauce; sweeter and less salty than soy sauce.

* Use a fair amount of salt, sea salt like Maldon or Fleur de Sel.

* Go with the garnishes (sesame seeds, sliced scallions), you won't miss the soy sauce.

How to Make Paleo Condiments:

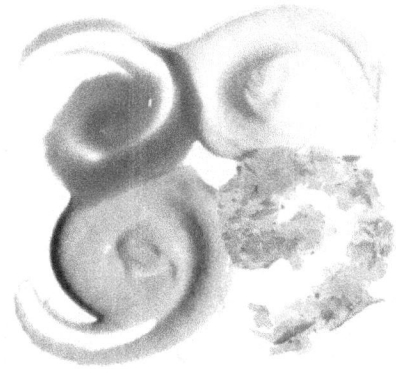

When switching to paleo, the things we miss the most are not so much the dairy, bread, pastries or breakfast cereals, but rather the small and flavorful additions we know as condiments.

I'm talking delicious food additions like ketchup, mustard, mayonnaise, horseradish, barbecue sauce and Worcestershire sauce.

Most store-bought condiments contain preservatives and HFCS or high-fructose corn syrup. Why not make my own.

Here is a short guide on how you can make delicious homemade paleo condiments with ingredients you probably already have in your kitchen.

Paleo Mayonaise #1

Ingredients:

1 pastured egg (works best if egg is allowed to set to room temperature)

1/2 tsp mustard powder

1 tsp lemon juice (fresh squeezed works best)

1/2 cup extra virgin olive oil

1/2 cup walnut oil (or another nut oil, or grapeseed- otherwise the EVOO flavor is very strong!)

Salt and pepper to taste

Directions:

In a food processor combine egg, mustard powder, and lemon juice until it reaches a thick, creamy consistency.

Slowly blend oil into egg mixture.

Add salt and pepper as desired.

Store in the refrigerator. Mayonnaise will thicken after a few hours.

Variations:

Chipotle: Use chopped chipotle peppers in adobo sauce. Add to desired level of spice. Great for dipping baked sweet potato fries.

Lemon-Dill: Add lemon zest and a generous amount of fresh dill. Great with salmon.

Roasted Garlic: Add 1-2 cloves of roasted garlic and freshly ground black pepper.

Herb: Play around with your favorite fresh herbs! This is an easy change that will make a world of flavor difference. Try fresh basil leaves and fresh cilantro (NOT together!)

Mayonnaise #2

Ingredients:

1 large egg

1 1/2 tablespoons lemon juice

1/2 teaspoon dry mustard

1/2 cup light olive oil

1/2 cup avocado oil

1/4 teaspoon ground white pepper (optional)
Directions:

Place egg, lemon juice, and mustard into a food processor.

Cover and blend until frothy; keep food processor running.

Drizzle in olive oil and avocado oil, drop by drop, through the drip hole in the top until smooth and creamy.

Season with white pepper.

Refrigerate in a sealed container.

Paleo Ketchup # 1

Ingredients:

2 (6 oz) cans tomato paste

1 cup of vegetable broth

¼ cup apple cider vinegar

1 tablespoon of onion powder

1 tablespoon of garlic powder

¼ teaspoon allspice or combine cinnamon, nutmeg and cloves

Sea or Himalayan salt to taste (add slowly)

* Not really strict Paleo but it works
Directions:

Blend together the tomato paste, vegetable broth, apple cider vinegar, and mix until blended well in a saucepan, and place it over a medium heat.

Add spices and salt slowly.

Let the mixture simmer on a low heat for 5-10 minutes.

Allow the sauce to cool completely.

Serve or place the mixture into an old ketchup container or glass that can be tightly sealed.

Ketchup #2

Ingredients:

1 12 oz can tomato paste

1 cup water

2 tbsp vinegar

½ tsp salt

½ tsp curry powder

½ tsp garlic powder

* Makes approximately 32 oz of ketchup, or 64 1tbsp servings.
Directions:

Blend and mix all ingredients in a sauce pan and bring to boil on medium-high heat.

Reduce heat to medium-low and simmer while stirring frequently until flavors have blended. (Add more water for thinner ketchup, add less water for thicker)

Transfer to a glass jar and cool before serving.

Homemade Paleo Worcestershire Sauce
Ingredients:

1/2 cup apple cider vinegar

2 tbsp water

2 tbsp soy sauce

1/4 tsp ground ginger

1/4 tsp mustard powder

1/4 tsp onion powder

1/4 tsp garlic powder

1/8 tsp cinnamon

1/8 tsp freshly ground black pepper
Directions:

In a saucepan combine all the ingredients and slowly bring to a bowl while frequently stirring.

Turn heat down and let simmer for about a minute for the flavors to set.

Cool and store in the refrigerator.

Simple Mustard

Ingredients:

1/2 cup mustard powder

1/2 cup water

Sea salt to taste
Directions:

Combine the mustard powder and water in a bowl and mix well.

Let the mustard stand for about 15 minutes before enjoying.

To add a little zing, try a bit of chopped fresh parsley or basil, lemon or lime zest and a tablespoon or two of your favorite vinegar.

Homemade Paleo Barbeque Sauce

Ingredients:

1/4 cup homemade ketchup

3 tbsp homemade mustard

1 tbsp Worcestershire sauce

1 onion, minced

1 clove garlic, minced

1 can (6 oz) tomato paste

1/2 cup apple cider vinegar

1/2 cup water

1 pinch ground cloves

1 pinch cinnamon

Smoked paprika to taste

Hot sauce to taste, optional

Directions:

In a cast-iron skillet, with a bit of cooking fat, brown the onion for about 4 minutes.

Include the garlic and cook for another minute.

Add all the other ingredients and simmer for 30 minutes.

Taste the sauce and adjust with more smoked paprika, vinegar or hot sauce to the desired taste.

Let barbeque sauce cool and Store in the refrigerator.

Hot Sauce

Ingredients:

1/2 cup extra virgin olive oil

6 jalapeno peppers, thinly sliced crosswise

6 cloves garlic, thinly sliced

1/2 cup fresh cilantro leaves, coarsely chopped
Directions:

Heat olive oil in a cast-iron skillet directly on the embers, on the side burner of a charcoal/gas grill, or on the stove.

When the oil is screaming hot, add the jalapenos, garlic, and cilantro.

Cook over high heat until the sauce is aromatic and the garlic is lightly browned, about 2 minutes.

Pour this sauce over steaks and serve.

Easy Paleo Horseradish

Ingredients:

1 cup peeled and minced horseradish root

3/4 cup white wine vinegar

1/4 tsp sea salt

Directions:

In a blender or food processor process all the ingredients to a paste.

Enjoy right away or store in the refrigerator.

Paleo Horseradish with a Twist

Ingredients:

3/4 lb horseradish root, minced

1 cup finely chopped beets

3/4 cup apple cider vinegar

1/2 tsp sea salt

Directions:

Process all the ingredients in a blender or food processor to a paste.

Enjoy right away or store in the refrigerator.

Breakfast

A lot of people get stuck in a breakfast rut (myself included) making the same dish every day. Most of us associate breakfast with cereal, toast, bagels, crumpets and sugar laden foods.

The Paleo Diet aims to remove these bad eating habits of the modern era we have developed through time, and replace it with the healthy way of eating that our ancestors had.

It's not really a problem finding Paleo slow cooker recipes for lunch and dinner, but when you eliminate grains, processed sugars, and most dairy, breakfast recipes are hard to come by. After all it is the most important meal of the day; therefore it is important to stick with your diet for the first meal of the day.

There is no breakfast rule declaring breakfast has to be full of grains and processed sugars. Who wants to start the day off with a big sugar crash anyway? Well, it's time to try something new for breakfast tomorrow!

Slow Cooker Sausage and Egg Soup

Ingredients:

1 lb ground pork

8 eggs, hard boiled, halved

1 onion, chopped

1 large can diced tomatoes

2 tbsp olive oil

4 cloves garlic minced

1 tsp thyme

1 tsp oregano

3 cups vegetable broth

¼ tsp chili flakes

1 bunch kale chopped

1 cup coconut milk

1 bunch chives
Directions:

Put the ground pork in the slow cooker.

In a skillet saute onions and garlic until translucent.

Combine all ingredients in the slow cooker except for coconut milk and kale.

Cook on low for 5-6 hrs.

10 minutes before crock pot has completed toss in coconut milk, hard boiled eggs, and kale. Stir and Garnish with chives.

Slow Cooker Breakfast Pie

Ingredients:

1lb pork sausage, broken up (veggie sausage or turkey sausage)

8 eggs, whisked

1 sweet potato or yam, shredded

1 yellow onion, diced

1 tablespoon garlic powder

2 teaspoons dried basil

salt and pepper, to taste

Throw in any extra veggies you have around: peppers, squash, etc.

Directions:

Lightly grease the inside of your slow cooker with coconut oil to make sure the egg doesn't stick to it.

Shred your sweet potato.

Add all ingredients to your cooker and use a spoon to mix well.

Place on low for 6-8 hours, or until pork sausage is completely cooked through.

Paleo Slow Cooker Breakfast Casserole with Sweet Potatoes

Ingredients:

Coconut Oil (grease inside of crock pot)

8 Eggs

2 Sweet Potatoes

2 Red Onions

2 Tablespoons Smoked Paprika

1 lb Meat of your choice
Directions:

Crack eggs and place in a bowl to set.

Cut sweet potatoes into cubes and put in the food processor along with two red onions.

Next place the sweet potatoes and onions into the slow cooker.

Whisk eggs in the bowl and add the paprika.

Blend meat you have chosen into the sweet potato and onion mixture; pour the eggs on top and mix all together in the cooker.

Cook on low heat for 4-6 hours.

Apple Breakfast Cobbler

Ingredients:

6 Apples, cored and sliced

1 T Coconut Oil

1/2 c Coconut Milk

1/2 c Shredded Coconut (unsweetened)

1/2 c Raisins (or any dried fruit)

1 T Cinnamon

1 t Salt

1 T Vanilla
Directions:

Grease the inside of your slow cooker with the coconut oil.

Place all other ingredients in a large mixing bowl and stir until combined.

Pour ingredients into the crockpot.

Cook on low for 6 hours or just overnight.

Serve topped with raw nuts and more coconut.

Ham Egg and Spinach Breakfast Casserole
Ingredients:

6 large eggs

1 teaspoon coconut oil

1/2 teaspoon salt

1/4 teaspoon black pepper

1/4 cup milk (almond milk, coconut milk, nut milk - Paleo)

1/2 coconut milk

1/2 teaspoon thyme

1/2 teaspoon portion of fresh onion

1 small pressed clove of garlic

1/3 cup diced mushrooms

1 cup (packed) baby spinach

1 cup shredded pepper jack cheese (for strict paleo use almond butter or eliminate)

1 cup ham, diced
Directions:

In a bowl combine and whisk the eggs, salt, pepper, milk, coconut milk, thyme, onion, garlic together until smooth.

Stir in the mushrooms, spinach, cheese, and ham.

Lightly coat the inside of a 6-Quart Slow Cooker with coconut oil.

Pour eggs mixture into the bottom of slow cooker.

Cover and cook on HIGH for 90 minutes-2 hours. Eggs should be set.

Slice and serve for breakfast.

Slow Cooker Paleo Banana Bread

Ingredients:

4 Small Ripe Bananas

1/4 Cup + 2 Tablespoons Melted Coconut Oil

1/2 Cup Honey

1 Tablespoon Vanilla

3 Tablespoons Coconut Milk

3 Eggs

2 Cups Almond Flour

1 teaspoon Baking Soda
Directions:

Mash the bananas in a large bowl.

Add in melted coconut oil.

Stir in Honey, Vanilla, Coconut Milk, and eggs. Mix well.

Add the flour and baking soda. (Mixture will be thin, like pancake batter)

Line slow cooker with parchment paper

Pour batter into slow cooker, cover, and cook on LOW for 2 hours.

Gluten Free Smoky Bacon Wraps

Ingredients:

1 teaspoon coconut oil

1 pkg bacon

1 pkg 16 oz miniature sausage links

1/2 Cup maple syrup

Directions:

Use the broiler or pan for a few minutes to crisp up the bacon.

Cut sausages in half. Take a strip of bacon and wrap around sausage.

One piece of bacon should be able to wrap around 3 pieces of sausage.

Coat inside of slow cooker with coconut oil and place wraps in cooker.

Put them as close together as possible and sprinkle with maple syrup.

Set slow cooker to HIGH and cook for 1 1/2 - 2 hours or until bacon is crisp.

Poultry

Slow Cooked Chicken Cacciatore

Ingredients:

3 lbs. cut up chicken

1 lg. onion, thinly sliced

2 (6 oz.) cans tomato paste (Use the same amount of tomato sauce instead)

4 oz. sliced mushrooms

1 tsp. salt

1 to 2 cloves garlic, minced

1 to 2 tsp. oregano

1/2 tsp. celery seed (I omit this)

1 bay leaf

1/2 cup of water

Directions:

Lay the sliced onions in bottom of slow cooker and add chicken pieces.

In a large bowl stir together remaining ingredients. Pour over chicken.

Cook on low 7 to 9 hours; or high 3 to 4 hours.

Hot and Zesty Lemon-Turmeric Chicken and Vegetables

Ingredients:

1 tablespoons turmeric

1 tablespoon ground cumin

1 tablespoon paprika

1 teaspoon cayenne pepper

1 teaspoon sea salt

1 whole lemon

3 1/2 lb. broiler/fryer chicken, skinned and trimmed of excess fat, rinsed and patted dry

1 large onion, chopped

5 cloves garlic, chopped

1/2 cup chopped cilantro

1 pound carrots, chopped

2 red bell peppers, chopped

1 can (14 ounces) fire roasted crushed tomatoes

1 teaspoon extra virgin olive oil
Directions:

Mix together the cayenne pepper, cumin, paprika, turmeric, and salt. From the whole lemon add the juice and and mix well; save the lemon rind.

Generously apply the spice mixture all over the inside and outside of the chicken.

The next step is to stuff the cavity of the chicken with half the onions, half of the garlic, and half of the cilantro.

With the remaining onions, garlic, cilantro, and place in the bottom of the slow cooker.

Add the crushed tomatoes, carrots, and bell pepper. Blend and Stir in the extra virgin olive oil. Season with salt to taste.

Place the chicken on top of the vegetables and cover.

Chicken can be cooked on low for about 7 hours or on high for approximately 4 hours

Crock Pot Italian Chicken

Ingredients:

12 boneless, skinless chicken thighs, cut into 1-inch pieces

2 14.5 oz cans tomatoes with Italian herbs

2 cups cubed zucchini

1 cup pearl onions, peeled

1 cup baby carrots

2 tablespoons tomato paste

4 cloves garlic, chopped

1 teaspoon raw honey

1 teaspoon red pepper flakes

Directions:

Combine all ingredients in crock pot. Stir to mix.

Cook on low setting 6 to 10 hours or until done.

Easy Whole Crockpot Chicken

Ingredients:

1 large chicken

1 onion

2 teaspoons paprika

1 teaspoon salt

1 teaspoon onion powder

1 teaspoon thyme

1/2 teaspoon garlic powder

1/4 teaspoon cayenne (red) pepper

1/4 teaspoon black pepper

Comments:

If your spice rack is stocked you'll hardly have to buy anything to make this. It is one of the best (and easiest) ways to slow cook a whole chicken until it is falling-off-the-bone tender and delicious.

Directions:

In a small bowl combine the dried spices.

Chop the onion and place it in the bottom of the slow cooker.

Remove giblets from chicken and then rub spice mixture all over, including inside the cavity and under the breast skin.

Place the prepared chicken on top of the onions in the cooker, and cover. No need to add any liquid.

Turn the slow cooker on high and cook for 4 - 5 hours (for a 3 or 4 pound chicken) or until the chicken meat is tender enough to fall off the bone.

Increase cooking time to 8-10 hours if chicken is over 6 lbs.

Paleo Slow Cooker Sicilian Hens

Ingredients:

2 Cornish hens, thawed, halved

1/4 cup toasted sliced almonds

3 tbsp drained capers

3 tbsp chopped fresh parsley

1 garlic clove, chopped

1/2 tsp paprika

2 tsp olive oil

1/4 tsp salt

1/8 tsp pepper

Chopped ripe olives

Directions:

Combine almonds, capers, parsley, garlic, paprika, oil, salt and pepper in a food processor with metal blades and finely chop.

Take the spice mixture and rub on all sides of Cornish hens.

Place on rack in slow cooker.

If all hens do not fit on rack, lightly cover halves with foil and arrange remaining halves on top.

Cook on low 7-8 hours.

Sprinkle with chopped olives. Makes 4 servings.

Sri Lankan Slowcooker Chicken

Ingredients:

5 chicken breasts

1 medium white onion, diced

1 knob of ginger, grated (about 2 tbsp)

4 thai chilis (I used two jalapenos and two serranos) - thinly sliced

4 cloves garlic

1 tbsp coriander

1 tsp turmeric

cayenne - a pinch if you like it mild up to 1/2 tbs to get it hot

1 tbsp curry powder (or 1/4 cup fresh curry leaves or 1 pandan leaf)

1 can coconut milk

2 tsp coconut oil

2 tbsp lemon juice

Directions:

Cook with a large skillet over medium-high heat (I use cast iron), saute your onions, peppers, and garlic in 2 tsp of coconut oil until the onion starts to become translucent.

Add spices and keep cooking until it becomes very aromatic with a little bit of a toasted smell.

Next take your vegetable and spice mixture and put into slowcooker. Also pour in one can of coconut milk and your lemon juice. Mix well.

Put the chicken breasts in the cooker and ladle a little of the sauce over the top.

Set on low and cook for 6 hours, or on high for 4 hours.

Chicken In A Pot

Ingredients:

3 lb whole chicken

2 carrots, sliced

2 onions, sliced

2 celery stalks with leaves, cut in 1 inch pieces

1 ts basil

1/2 ts salt

1/2 ts black pepper

1/2 c chicken broth

Directions:

Place the carrots, onions, and celery in the bottom of crock-pot.

Add whole chicken on top with salt, pepper, liquid. Sprinkle a little basil over top.

Cover the slow cooker and cook until done-low 8 to 10 hours. (High 3 to 4 hours, using 1 cup water).

Remove chicken and vegetables and serve.

Crock Pot Chicken Recipe

Ingredients:

1 chicken

2 carrots, sliced thinly

2 md onions, sliced thinly

2 celery stalks with leaves, chopped

1/2 t salt

1/2 t black pepper

16 oz chicken broth

2 c water

1 t basil, crushed

1 t oregano

1 t garlic powder

Directions:

Pour half of the chicken broth, half of the carrots, celery and onions in the bottom of the crock pot.

With back side down of the chicken facing down put the chicken in the slow cooker.

Squeeze in the remaining broth, vegetables, salt and pepper, basil, oregano and garlic, around the chicken.

Place the lid on cooker and cook on low heat for 7-10 hours or HIGH heat for 2 1/2 to 3 1/2 hours.

Honey Garlic Chicken Wings

Ingredients:

2-3 lb of wings (approx. 20-30 wings)

3/4 cup of raw honey (preferably liquid or melted)

1.5 tbsp of minced garlic

2 tbsp of olive oil

1/2 tsp sea salt

1/2 tsp pepper
Directions:

Combine honey, garlic, olive oil, salt and pepper until liquid.

To soften the honey, heat ingredients on the stove to soften.

Place wings in your crockpot.

Pour ingredients over wings; stir so the sauce covers the wings completely.

Cook on low for 6 hours or 3-4 hours on high.

Jamaican Jerk Chicken Wings

Ingredients:

3 to 4 pounds of chicken wings or drumsticks, browned

2 Tbsp Jamaican Jerk seasoning.

Juice of one large orange (about 1/4 cup).

Juice of one small lime.

2 Tbsp coconut aminos or wheat free tamari.

1 Tbsp apple cider vinegar.

1 Tbsp coconut sap crystals (optional).

Directions:

In a skillet slightly brown your chicken pieces.

Rub your wings with your jerk seasoning so that they are evenly coated.

In a bowl mix your remaining ingredients.

Place your seasoned chicken into a large plastic bag and then dump in your marinade.

Make sure wings are evenly coated and let sit in the fridge overnight.

Coat inside of slow cooker with coconut oil and cook on high for 2 hours or low for 4 hours.

Paleo Style Buffalo Wings

Ingredients:

4 ounces of grass fed butter. Paleo substitute ghee or 1/3 cup of coconut oil.

1/2 cup Frank's Red Hot sauce, plus another 1/4 cup set aside.

3 to 4 pounds of chicken wings or drumsticks, browned.

Directions:

In the broiler or pan, brown your chicken pieces.

Melt your butter (or ghee or coconut oil) and mix with 1/2 cup of the hot sauce.

Place your wings in your slow cooker and pour your butter and hot sauce mixture over the chicken and make sure the pieces are evenly coated.

Add the extra 1/4 cup of hot sauce directly onto the chicken pieces.

Cook on high for 2 hours or low for 4 hours.

Tip: Prep your wings ahead of time and let them marinate in the fridge overnight before cooking.

Honey Turkey with Orange Cranberry Sauce

Ingredients:

1/4 cup honey.

1 tablespoon cornstarch. (arrowroot to use as a thickening agent)

3/4 cup orange marmalade.

1 cup fresh cranberries, ground or finely chopped.

1 small boneless turkey breast, about 3 to 4 pounds.

Salt and pepper to taste.

Directions:

In small saucepan, blend sugar and arrowroot; stir in marmalade and cranberries.

Cook over medium heat, stirring, until mixture is bubbly and slightly thickened.

Place turkey breast in slow cooker. Sprinkle all over with salt and pepper.

Pour the sauce over turkey. Cover and cook on HIGH for 1 hour.

Reduce heat to LOW and cook 6 to 8 hours longer.

An instant-read thermometer should register about 175°. Slice turkey and serve with sauce.

Slow Cooked Turkey With Sweet Potatoes

Ingredients:

3 medium sweet potatoes peeled and cut into 2-inch cubes

1 1/2 to 2 pounds turkey thighs, skin removed

1 1/2 to 2 cups turkey gravy

2 tbsp. coconut or almond flour

1 tsp. dried parsley

1/2 teaspoon dried rosemary crushed

1/4 teaspoon dried leaf thyme

1/8 tsp. pepper

1 1/2 to 2 cups frozen cut green beans

Directions:

Layer sweet potatoes and turkey in slow cooker.

Combine gravy, flour, parsley, rosemary, thyme, and pepper; stir until smooth.

Pour gravy mixture over the turkey and sweet potatoes.

Cover and cook on high for 1 hour. Reduce heat to low and cook 5 hours longer.

Stir in green beans. Cover and cook 1 to 2 hours until turkey is tender and juices run clear.

Remove turkey and vegetables to a serving dish with a slotted spoon. Stir sauce and serve with turkey and vegetables.

Serves 6

Slow and Easy Turkey Barbecue

Ingredients:

2 to 3 pounds turkey cutlets or chops

2 green bell peppers, or combination of red, yellow, and green, cut in strips

1 teaspoon celery salt

Dash of pepper

1 to 2 tablespoons finely chopped onion, or 2 teaspoons dried minced onion

2 cups thick barbecue sauce

Directions:

Sprinkle turkey cutlets with salt and pepper; cover and bake in 350° oven for 1 hour. Uncover for desired darker color.

Meanwhile, combine barbecue sauce and celery salt in 5 quart slow cooker. Add green peppers and onions.

Cover and cook on high while turkey is baking.

Chop turkey (as desired in small to medium chunks) and add to slow cooker/Crock Pot.

Cover and cook on low for 4 hours or HIGH for 2 hours. Serve with fresh split rolls. Turkey recipe serves 4 to 6.

Beef - Pork - Lamb

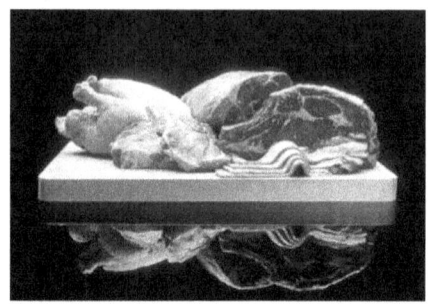

Slow Cooker Paleo Pot Roast

Ingredients:

3 lbs chuck roast

3 tablespoons coconut oil

2 cup chopped carrots

2 lbs chopped parsnips

1 onion sliced

2 cloves garlic chopped

2 cups beef broth

Directions:

Lightly coat the inside of the your slow cooker with coconut oil.

In a large skillet heat the remaining coconut oil.

Add the roast, seasoned with salt and pepper, to the skillet.

Get a good Sear on both sides.

In the bottom of the crock pot place vegetables; pour the cooking stock in, and add the roast on top.

Cover and cook on low for 10-12 hours until roast is tender.

Serve with vegetables.

Slow Cooker Pork Loin
Ingredients:

2 pounds boneless pork loin, cut into 1-inch cubes

1/2 cup orange juice

1 tablespoon curry powder

1 teaspoon chicken bouillon granules

1/2 teaspoon ground ginger

1/4 teaspoon ground cinnamon

1/2 teaspoon salt

1 tart apple, peeled and diced

1 small onion, chopped

1 clove garlic, minced

1/4 cup raisins

1/4 cup flaked coconut

2 tablespoons cold water

2 tablespoons potato starch(arrowroot)
Directions:

In a slow cooker combine orange juice, curry powder, chicken bouillon, ginger, cinnamon, and salt.

Next stir the apple, onion, garlic, raisins, and coconut into the cooker.

Place pork cubes in the sauce.

Then, in a small dish, whisk together the water and potato starch until there are no lumps; stir into slow cooker.

Cover the cooker; select a low setting and cook until pork is very tender, 5 to 6 hours.

Apple Glazed Pork Roast (Slow Cooker)
Ingredients:

3-4 lb. pork loin roast (well trimmed)

salt and pepper

4-6 apples, cored and quartered (peeled, optional)

1/4 cup apple juice (fresh squeezed for paleo)

2 Tbsp. raw honey

1 tsp. ginger
Directions:

First, rub roast with salt and pepper.

To remove excess fat, brown roast under broiler, drain well.

Put the apple quarters in bottom of slow cooker and place roast on top of apples.

Combine the rest of ingredients in the cooker; spoon over roast.

Cook on low for 10-12 hours.

Slow Cooker Pear Ginger Pork Chops

Ingredients:

4 thick cut pork chops

2 tablespoons coconut oil

1/2 teaspoon cinnamon

1 teaspoon allspice

2 ripe d'anjou pears, cored and cut into chunks

2 tablespoons apple cider vinegar (apple juice)

1 cup white wine (can substitute water or broth)

2 tablespoons honey

1 tablespoon fresh ginger, minced

Salt and pepper just before serving
Directions:

In a cast-iron skillet over medium heat, melt 1 tablespoon of the coconut oil.

Brown the pork chops on both sides for about 5 minutes total and place in the slow cooker.

Sauté the pears and ginger in the remaining coconut oil.

Add the vinegar and wine, turn to medium low and cook for 5 minutes to reduce slightly.

Pour mixture over chops in slow cooker.

Cook on low for 6 hours.

Salt and pepper to taste, then serve.

Leg of Lamb Cooked Slow with Rosemary Lemon & Garlic

Ingredients:

1 leg of lamb that will fit in your CrockPot

1 lemon

4-5 garlic cloves, sliced or crushed

1 Tbsp. fresh rosemary, chopped

1 Tbsp. olive oil

1/2 tsp. coarse salt

1 tsp. freshly ground black pepper

Wine, chicken or beef stock, tomato juice or water
Directions:

Prep the meat by patting your lamb dry with paper towels.

If you don't have a mortar and pestle, find a way to finely grate about half the zest off the lemon and grind into a paste with the garlic, rosemary, oil, salt and pepper.

Then, rub the paste all over the lamb.

If you like, let it sit for half an hour or so; refrigerate for a few hours or overnight.

Put it into the slow cooker.

Add about half a cup of liquid and squeeze the juice of the lemon over-top.

Cover and cook on low for 6-8 hours.

Paleo Jamaican Beef Pepper Pot

Ingredients:

2-lb stewing beef cubes

2-sweet potatoes, peeled and cubed

1-tbsp coconut or macadamia oil

8-slices bacon, chopped

2-onions, chopped

4-cloves garlic, minced

6-cups beef stock

1/4-cup tomato paste

1-tsp dried thyme

1/2-tsp salt

1-tsp pepper

1-sweet red pepper, chopped

1-green pepper, chopped

1-tbsp lemon or lime juice

1-tbsp hot pepper sauce
Directions:

Put sweet potatoes in bottom of slow cooker.

Over a high heat, using a saucepan or Dutch oven, heat oil; brown beef in batches.

Add to slow cooker.

Cook and crisp bacon in saucepan; over a medium heat. Drain off fat.

Add onions and garlic to sauce pan with bacon; cook, stirring occasionally until softened, about 5 minutes.

Add stock, 1 1/2-cups water, tomato paste, thyme, salt and pepper to the saucepan; bring to boil.

Pour into slow cooker.

Cover and cook on low for 8-10 hours or until beef and sweet potatoes are *tender.*

Add the red and green peppers.

Cover and cook on high for 15 minutes.

Stir in citrus juice and hot pepper sauce.

Malaysian Slow Cooked Beef Curry

Ingredients:

Spice Paste

4 - 8 large dried New Mexico chiles

2 - 4 lemongrass talks

1/2 c onions, chopped

6 cloves garlic, peeled

2 t coriander

1 1 /2 t cumin

1/2 t ginger

3 T pure fish sauce (Red Boat Fish Sauce)

Optional Ingredients:

Stew
--

3 lb boneless chuck roast or stew meat, trimmed, and cut into 1 1/2" cubes

1 (13.5-oz) can unsweetened coconut milk

zest from 1 lime

2 whole star anise

1 cinnamon stick

1 T tamarind paste

chopped fresh cilantro

Directions:

Spice paste: Cover the chiles with very hot water and soak until soft, about 45 minutes.

Drain chiles, stem, seed, and chop. Cut off the bottom 4" from the lemongrass stalks.

In a food processor chop lemongrass bottoms and chiles (reserve tops of stalks for the stew).

To the food processor add onions, garlic, coriander, cumin, ginger, 1 t black pepper and process until finely ground.

Add the 1/2 cup of water, chiles, and fish sauce. Process to paste.

Stew: Mash reserved lemongrass stalks with a rolling pan.

Bend in half and bundle with kitchen twine.

In the slow cooker mix beef and spice paste and stir in lemongrass bundles, coconut milk, lime zest, star anise, cinnamon, and tamarind.

Press meat down completely to submerge.

On low heat setting cook stew until meat is very tender, 4 1/2 - 5 hours.

Remove lemongrass bundles, stir anise, and cinnamon stick.

Serve over top steamed rice and sprinkled with cilantro.

Corned Beef and Cabbage Paleo Friendly

Ingredients:

2-3 lb. corned beef brisket with seasoning packet

6 organic carrots, cut into chunks

2 organic onions, chopped

1 organic cabbage, wedged

2-3 cups water

Directions:

Combine carrots, onions, and cabbage in 4-6 quart Crockpot.

Under cold running water rinse-off corned beef and pat dry with paper towels.

Sprinkle with contents of seasoning mix and place corned beef in crockpot.

Pour the 2-3 cups of water over corned beef.

Cover slow cooker and cook on low setting for 8-9 hours.

Remove corned beef and vegetables from cooker and cover; put into 200 degree oven to keep warm, if needed!

Serving Suggestions:

Cut corned beef across grain into thin slices.

Place corned beef slices over vegetables from crockpot. Serve cooking juices over the food.

Serve with paleo mustard on the side

Slow Cooker Honey Barbecue Pork Spare Ribs

Ingredients:

Homemade Paleo Barbecue Sauce:

Cooking oil of your choice

1 cup minced fresh onion

1 teaspoon sea salt

4 cloves garlic, minced

1 tsp ground cumin

1 tsp dry mustard

1 tsp dried basil

1 tsp dried oregano

½ tsp cayenne

1 cup tomato paste

1 ½ cups homemade chicken broth

2 tablespoons raw apple cider vinegar

2 tablespoons honey
Ingredients:

3-4 lbs pork spare ribs

Salt and pepper to taste
Directions:

How to make homemade barbeque sauce: heat oil and onions in a large saucepan over medium heat. Stir until tender, about 10 to 15 minutes.

To the saucepan add herbs, spices, and remaining ingredients; whisk until smooth. Bring to a low boil.

Salt and pepper spare ribs and arrange in your slow cooker.

Next pour the sauce over the meat and cook on low for 8 hours, or until the meat is tender and beginning to fall apart.

Serve ribs with sweet potato fries or vegetables.

Crockpot Coffee Braised Chile Beef

Ingredients:

1 beef roast (Eye of round roast, Brisket works, or chuck roast for a fattier cut)

4 garlic cloves, minced or pressed

2 tsp cocoa powder

3 Tbs ancho chile powder

1 tsp oregano (preferably Mexican oregano)

1/8 tsp cinnamon

1 tsp cumin

1/2 tsp chipotle powder (optional; if you like spicy food)

1/2 tsp salt, or to taste

3/4 cup strong brewed coffee, preferably cold brewed

1 Tbs balsamic vinegar

Half a large red onion, thickly sliced

Optional **Ingredients:**

For a pre-made spice mix use VSpicery Cocoa Loco or Penzeys Chili 9000 instead of the spice mix. Just season the roast liberally and braise in the coffee-vinegar mixture.

Directions:

Combine all ingredients, except for the beef, coffee, onion, and vinegar, and add enough water to form a loose paste.

Rub beef with the spice paste on all sides.

Spread the onion in the bottom of your slow cooker.

Place the beef roast on top.

Stir the vinegar into the coffee and pour it over the roast.

Cook for 6-8 hours on low or until very tender.

Simple Crockpot Barbecued Spareribs

Ingredients:

4 pounds pork spareribs, cut in serving-size pieces

Salt and pepper, or seasoned salt and pepper

1 medium onion

1 bottle (16 ounces) barbecue sauce, or 2 cups of homemade barbecue sauce

Directions:

Sprinkle ribs with salt and pepper; place on broiler rack.

Broil ribs for 20 to 25 minutes.

Place ribs in slow cooker along with sliced onion and barbecue sauce.

Cover and cook on LOW for 6 to 8 hours.

Serves 4 to 6.

Slow Cooked Fruited Pork

Ingredients:

2 pounds pork boneless loin roast

1 1/2 cup mixed dried fruit

1/2 cup apple juice

1/2 teaspoon salt

1/4 teaspoon black pepper
Directions:

Place pork in 3-4 quart slow cooker and top with fruit.

Pour apple juice over pork and sprinkle with salt and pepper.

Cover crockpot and cook on low for 7-9 hours until pork is tender.

Pulled Pork Crockpot Recipe

Ingredients:

Pork shoulder

1 cup water

Basil

Rosemary

BBQ sauce (Paleo barbeque sauce)
Directions:

Cook the pork shoulder roast in the crockpot overnight on low with 1 cup of water and some basil and rosemary.

In the morning turn cooker off and let it cool down a bit. Remove any skin or bone.

Pull the meat apart into small pieces and return it to the crockpot.

Dump in BBQ sauce and a little water (1/4 c.) and mix it all together. Put it back on low for a few hours.

Irish Lamb Stew -- Crockpot Recipe

Ingredients:

1-2 pounds lamb, cut up (or broth, bones and leftovers from above recipe)

3-4 yellow onions, cut into 1/2" pieces

6-8 carrots, cut into 1/2" slices

3-4 cloves garlic, chopped (omit if using garlicky leftovers from above)

1-2 bay leaves

1/2-1 t. dried tarragon

1/2-1 t. ground black pepper

Directions:

Combine the above ingredients in a crockpot with enough water to barely cover.

Cook overnight on low (slower cooking lets the veggies flavor through without getting mushy).

Allow to cool in order to easily remove the excess fat, the bones, and the bay leaves.

Reheat to serve.

Paleo Slow Cooker Lamb Vindaloo

Ingredients:

3 lbs boneless leg of lamb (unless you can find lamb stew meat)

2 T dried minced onion (or 1 medium yellow onion, minced)

6 cloves of minced garlic

1/2 t ground clove

1 t ground ginger

3/4 t red cayenne pepper (+/-)

1 T ground coriander

1 T cumin

1 t cinnamon

1/4 cup lemon or lime juice

optional: 1 can tomatoes [or 1/2 cup water]
Directions:

Carefully trim the lamb, and cut into stew-meat sized chunks.

Put in slow cooker with all of the dry spices and onion.

Let it sit overnight in the fridge.

This could be optional, but having the meat soak up the spice flavor is the key to making a really good vindaloo.

In the morning add the 1/4 cup of citrus juice.

Add the can of tomatoes or 1/2 cup of water.

Cook on low for 8-10 hours.

Slow Cooker Italian Beef Sandwiches

Ingredients:

2 1/2 lbs grass fed beef chuck roast

1 tsp dried basil

1 tsp dried oregano

1 tsp dried crushed rosemary

1 tsp garlic powder

1 tsp onion powder

1/4-1/2 tsp salt

1/4 tsp black pepper

1/2 cup water

1 Tbsp red wine vinegar

2 Tbsp Dijon mustard

6 large portobella mushroom caps

Directions:

In a large skillet, heat 1 tablespoon of oil.

Combine all the spices together and rub them onto the beef roast.

In the skillet sear the roast on both sides for about 4-5 minutes per side.

Put the roast in the slow cooker and add the water and red wine vinegar.

Cook for 7-8 hours on low setting.

Remove roast and shred the meat.

Skim-off any fat in the crock pot and then add the Dijon mustard. Stir to combine.

Add the shredded beef back to the crock pot for juices to set.

For serving use portobella mushroom "buns" (Drizzle with oil, salt, and pepper and roasted for about 10 minutes at 450 F)

Serve with side of roasted cauliflower, carrots, and zucchini.

Seafood

Paleo Jambalaya Crockpot Soup

Ingredients:

1 lb large shrimp, raw and de-veined.

4 oz. chicken, diced

5 c. chicken stock.

4 peppers – any color you want, chopped

1 large onion, chopped

1 large can of organic diced tomatoes (leave the juice)

2 cloves garlic, diced

2 bay leafs

1 pkg spicy Andouille sausage

1/2-1 head of cauliflower

2 c. okra (optional)

3 tbsp Cajun Seasoning

1/4 c. Red Hot

Optional Ingredients:

Make Your Own Cajun Seasoning:

2 1/2 tablespoons paprika

2 tablespoons salt

2 tablespoons garlic powder

1 tablespoon black pepper

1 tablespoon onion powder

1 tablespoon cayenne pepper

1 tablespoon dried oregano

1 tablespoon dried thyme

(Yields about 2/3 c.)
Directions:

Put in the crockpot the chopped peppers, onions, garlic, chicken, cajun seasoning, Red Hot, and bay leafs with the chicken stock.

Set the cooker on low and cook for 6 hours.

About 1/2 hour before it's finished, toss in the cut up sausages.

While cooking make cauliflower rice by pulsing raw cauliflower in the food processor until it resembles rice.

For the last 20 minutes of the cooking time, add in the cauliflower rice and the raw shrimp.

Note: You can choose to quickly steam the cauliflower rice in the microwave and serve the jambalaya OVER it as well.

Key West Slow Cooker Citrus Fish

Ingredients:

1 1/2 pounds fish fillets

Salt and pepper to taste

1/2 cup chopped onion

5 tablespoons chopped fresh parsley

2 tablespoons coconut oil

2 teaspoons grated lemon rind

2 teaspoons grated orange rind

Orange and lemon slices, for garnish

Parsley sprigs, for garnish
Directions:

Grease inside of slow cooker with 1 tbs of the coconut oil.

Sprinkle fish fillets with salt and pepper.

Place fish in cooker. Put onion, parsley, grated orange and lemon rind, and remaining coconut oil over fish.

Cover and cook on LOW for 1 1/2 hours.

Manhattan Clam Chowder

Ingredients:

5 to 6 sliced bacon, diced

1 cup chopped onion

2 carrots, thinly sliced

3 ribs celery with leaves, thinly sliced

1 tablespoon fresh parsley, or 1 teaspoon dried

1 large can (28 ounces) tomatoes, broken up, undrained (or 2 large fresh tomatoes)

1 1/2 tsp. salt

black pepper

1 bay leaf

1 tsp. dried thyme

3 medium sweet potatoes, diced

2 or 3 cans (6 to 7 oz each) minced clams with juice

1 bottle (8oz) clam juice

1 tablespoon almond flour blended with 1 tablespoon melted butter or a little of the bacon grease, optional
Directions:

In a cast iron skillet or pan, fry diced bacon until crispy; drain and transfer to 3 1/2-quart or larger slow cooker.

Add remaining ingredients to the cooker; stir to blend.

Cover and cook on low for 8 to 10 hours. If a thicker soup is desired, add flour butter mixture during the last 30 minutes.

Serves 4.

Crockpot Fish Chowder

Ingredients:

2 pounds frozen fish filets (catfish, haddock, striped bass, etc.)

1/4 lb. bacon or salt pork, diced

1 medium onion, chopped

4 medium sweet potatoes, peeled and cubed

2 cups water

1 to 1 1/2 teaspoons salt, or to taste

1/4 tsp. pepper

1 can (12 ounces) evaporated milk or substitute (almond milk, coconut milk, nut milk)

Directions:

Thaw frozen fish in refrigerator. Cut into bite-sized pieces.

In skillet, saute bacon or salt pork and onion until meat is cooked and onion is golden.

Drain and put into crock pot with the fish pieces.

Add potatoes, water, salt and pepper.

Cover and cook on low for 5 to 8 hours.

Add evaporated milk or (coconut milk) during last hour.

Florida Keys Fisherman's Stew

Ingredients:

1 large can (28 ounces) crushed tomatoes with juice or (2 large fresh tomatoes)

1 can (8 ounces) tomato sauce

1/2 cup chopped onion

1 cup dry white wine or (fruit juice)

1/3 cup olive oil

3 cloves garlic, minced

1/2 cup parsley, chopped

1 green pepper, chopped

1 hot pepper (optional), chopped

salt and pepper, to taste

1 teaspoon thyme

2 teaspoons basil

1 teaspoon oregano

1/2 teaspoon paprika

1/2 teaspoon cayenne pepper

water, if desired*

Seafood

1 deboned (important) and cubed fillet of mahi-mahi, snapper, hog fish or seabass, cod or any whitefish.

1 doz. prawns

1 doz. scallops

1 doz. mussels

1 doz. clams (can use canned)
Directions:

Place all ingredients in slow cooker except seafood.

Cover and cook 6 to 8 hours on low.

About 30 minutes before serving, add your seafood.

Turn the heat up to HIGH and stir occasionally (but gently).

**Use your imagination and personal preferences as to which seafoods to add. Some choose to serve with fresh stone crab when in season.

Slow Cooked Shrimp Creole

Ingredients:

1 1/2 cups diced celery

1 1/4 c. chopped onion

1 c. chopped bell pepper

1 (8 oz.) can tomato sauce

1 (28 oz.) can whole tomatoes, broken up (2 large fresh tomatoes)

1 clove garlic, minced

1 tsp. salt

1/4 tsp. pepper

6 drops Tabasco, or to taste

1 lb. shrimp, deveined & shelled

Directions:

Combine all ingredients except shrimp and cook 3 to 4 hours on high or 6 to 8 hours on low.

Add shrimp last hour of cooking.

Chicken, rabbit or crawfish may be substituted for shrimp.

Crock Pot Shrimp Marinara Sauce

Ingredients:

1 (14.5 oz.) can of diced tomatoes

2 tbsp. minced fresh parsley

1 clove of garlic, minced

1/2 tsp. dried leaf basil

1 tsp. salt

1/4 tsp. pepper

1 tsp. dried oregano

1 (6 oz.) can tomato paste

1/2 tsp. seasoned salt

1 lb. cooked shelled shrimp

Grated Parmesan cheese (eliminate for strict Paleo)

Steamed vegetables

Directions:

In a slow cooker, combine tomatoes with parsley, garlic, basil, salt, pepper, oregano, tomato paste and seasoned salt.

Cover and cook on low for 6 to 7 hours.

Turn control to high, stir in the cooked shrimp, cover and cook on high for about 15 minutes longer.

Serve over steamed vegetables. Top with Parmesan cheese or serve it on the side.

Serves 4.

Crock Pot Fish Au Gratin

Ingredients:

3 pounds frozen white fish fillets, thawed

6 tablespoons butter (coconut oil, olive oil, bacon grease)

3 tablespoons coconut flour

1 1/2 teaspoon salt

1/2 tablespoon dry mustard

1/4 tablespoon nutmeg

1 1/4 cup coconut milk

1 1/2 teaspoon lemon juice

1 cup Cheddar cheese, shredded (Coconut milk flavored with a bit of honey or orange zest, chilled)
Directions:

Melt butter or substitute in saucepan on medium heat.

Stir in flour, salt, mustard and nutmeg.

Gradually add milk, stirring constantly until thickened.

Add lemon juice and cheese. Stir until cheese is melted.

Place fish into crock pot, spooning sauce over fish to cover.

Cover and cook on high 1 to 1-1/2 hours or until fish flakes.

Appetizers

Slow Cooker Sweet and Sour Meatballs

Ingredients:

1 plastic slow cooker liner

1 (9- to 10-ounce) jar sweet and sour sauce

1/4 cup light brown sugar(Use *half the amount called for, or substitute maple syrup)*

3 tablespoons soy sauce (Coconut animos or fish sauce)

1/2 teaspoon garlic powder (garlic clove)

1/2 teaspoon black pepper

2 1/2 pounds frozen meatballs

1 red bell pepper, chopped

1 (20-ounce) can pineapple chunks, drained

Directions:

Place liner in a slow cooker bowl, fitting it snugly against bottom and sides of bowl; pull top of liner over bowl rim.

Place all ingredients in slow cooker; stir gently then cover with lid. Cook on low setting for 7 to 8 hours, or on high setting for 4 to 5 hours, until done.

Carefully remove lid to allow steam to escape. Serve directly from slow cooker.

www.ingramcontent.com/pod-product-compliance
Lightning Source LLC
Chambersburg PA
CBHW071442070526
44578CB00001B/203